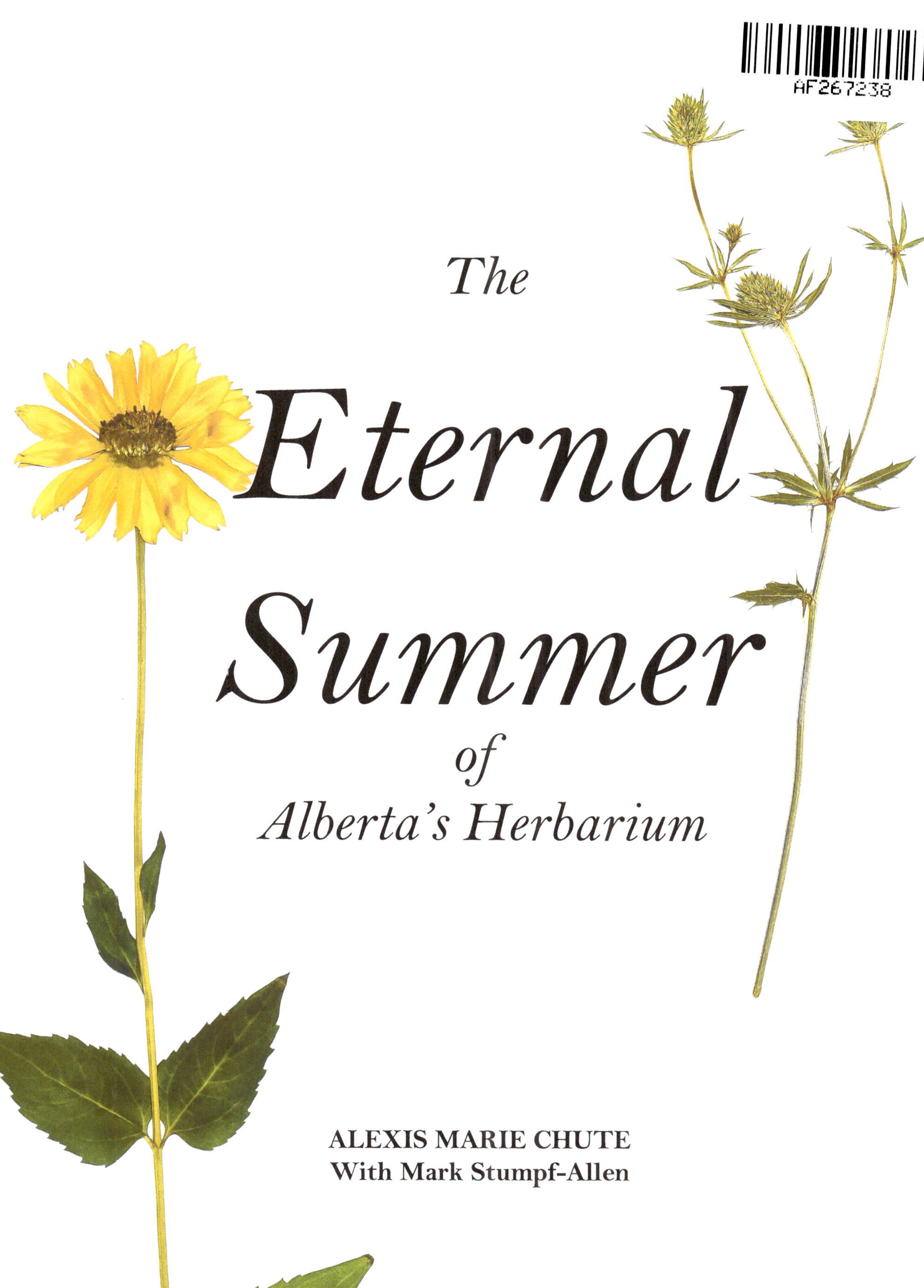

The *Eternal Summer*

of
Alberta's Herbarium

ALEXIS MARIE CHUTE
With Mark Stumpf-Allen

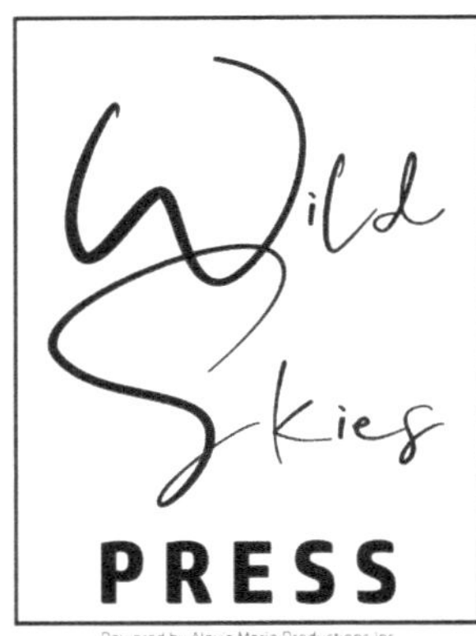

Copyright © Alexis Marie Chute

Published 2022
Printed in Canada

ISBN Hardcover 978-0-9950788-4-0
ISBN Paperback 978-1-0693754-2-1

Cover Design by Alexis Marie Chute
Interior Design by Alexis Marie Chute

For information address:
Wild Skies Press
A division of Alexis Marie Productions Inc.
Edmonton, Alberta, Canada
info@alexismariechute.com
www.WildSkiesPress.com

Wild Skies Press is an independent literary publisher founded in 2021. Wild Skies refers to the aurora borealis—northern lights—in Alberta, where the press is located, situated on Treaty 6 Territory. Wild Skies Press publishes non-fiction, fiction, poetry, and hybrid genres with an emphasis on the creation of Canadian works and books by emerging and established authors.

www.WildSkiesPress.com

*"Don't worry about the details,
focus on the Big Truths!"*

– Mark Stumpf-Allen

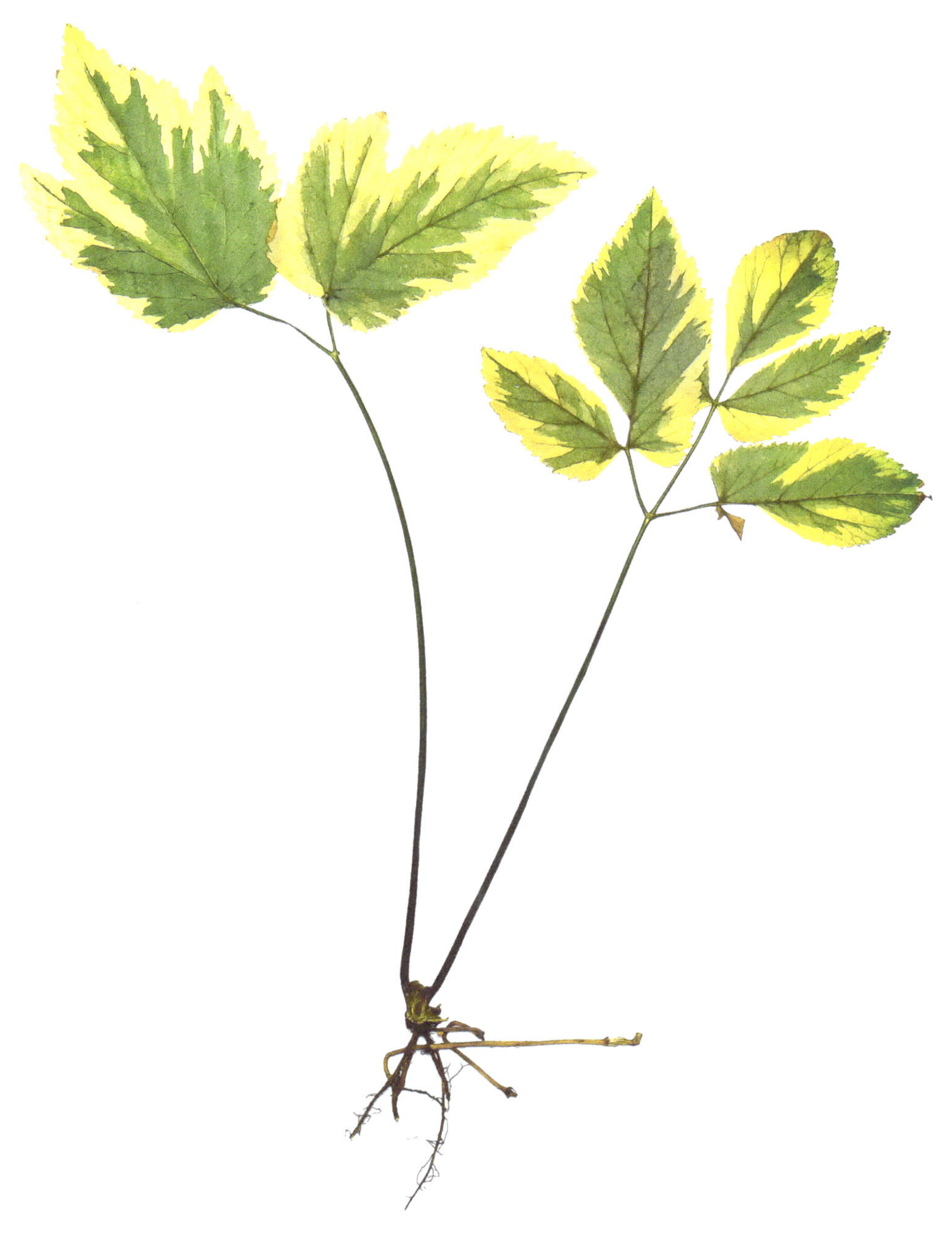

A Closer Look at the Natural World

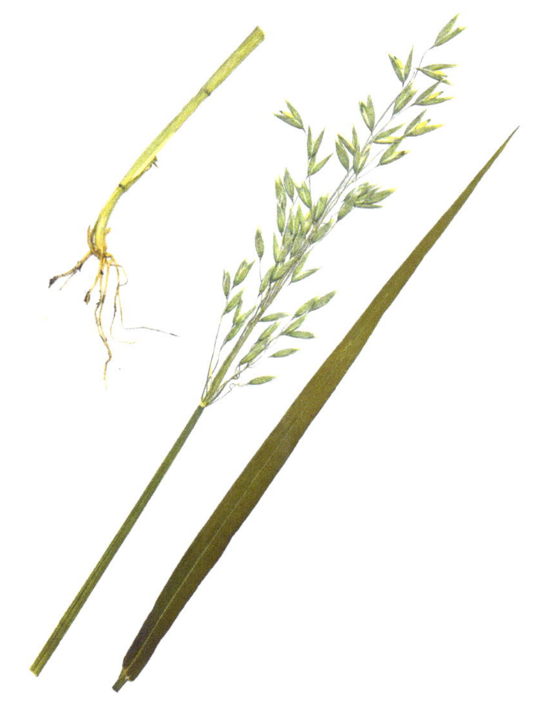

*"Study nature, love nature,
stay close to nature.
It will never fail you."*

– Frank Lloyd Wright

How do you capture a moment, a journey, a relationship?

Plants intersect with our lives in joyful ways. They are expressions of affection. They're in our favourite meals, provide our summer shade, and are the backdrop of our tropical vacations. We appreciate their beauty and their resiliency.

From an early age, pressing leaves in books is a wondrous activity. Children are natural scientists: making observations of colour, shape, texture, and fragrance. As we grow, it can be meditative, nostalgic, and sometimes therapeutic to tend a garden or simply admire a bouquet of fresh flowers. In both science and art, our relationship to nature is profound.

The herbarium specimens in *Eternal Summer* were created by master gardener students at the Multicultural Heritage Centre. Of the nine assignments in the Organic Master Gardener Program, OMG for short, creating an herbarium is the most daunting. Students assemble a portfolio of at least ten plant samples. These plants are collected, recorded, pressed, and mounted to become a record of what grew in their Alberta neighbourhoods. Since the program began in 2007, more than a thousand herbarium specimens have been completed.

This assignment is not intended to test students' crafting skills. The purpose of an herbarium in scientific study is to record observations about the plant's characteristics and community, learn taxonomy and plant identification, and better understand related studies like plant/insect relationships, adaptation, and phenology and distribution.

The goal is to reconnect the adult student with their inner child, the scientist. With modern aids—a simple loupe (a set of small magnifying glasses for observing fine details) or going as far as DNA analysis—we learn even more about the world around us. The assignment can take between ten hours and several years. For the student, this is a personal journey. Their specimens are brought out to show friends, framed to decorate their walls, or occasionally presented as gifts to mentors and loved ones.

As the Multicultural Heritage Centre builds its botanical collection of living plants, it will also preserve the history of what grew there. These important botanical records help us better understand our world, document ecology, and track how plant populations adapt to changing conditions. Some larger herbariums, specimens hundreds of years old, continue to inform our knowledge of nature. Almost all the information needed is presented on the specimen—it's as close as we get to being in the time and place where the plant was collected.

An herbarium specimen can represent many things: a record of adventure, a piece of wall art, or the beginning of a collection of curiosities.

Learning to create your own herbarium is simple, and anyone can build on these skills and have the data become part of an established regional herbarium record. Your work may inform future scientists of what Alberta was like in this time of rapid change and adaptation. A healthy way to adapt to change is to be a part of it.

Plant pressing offers us a gateway to reconnect with our world and integrate nature into our lives with greater intention and care.

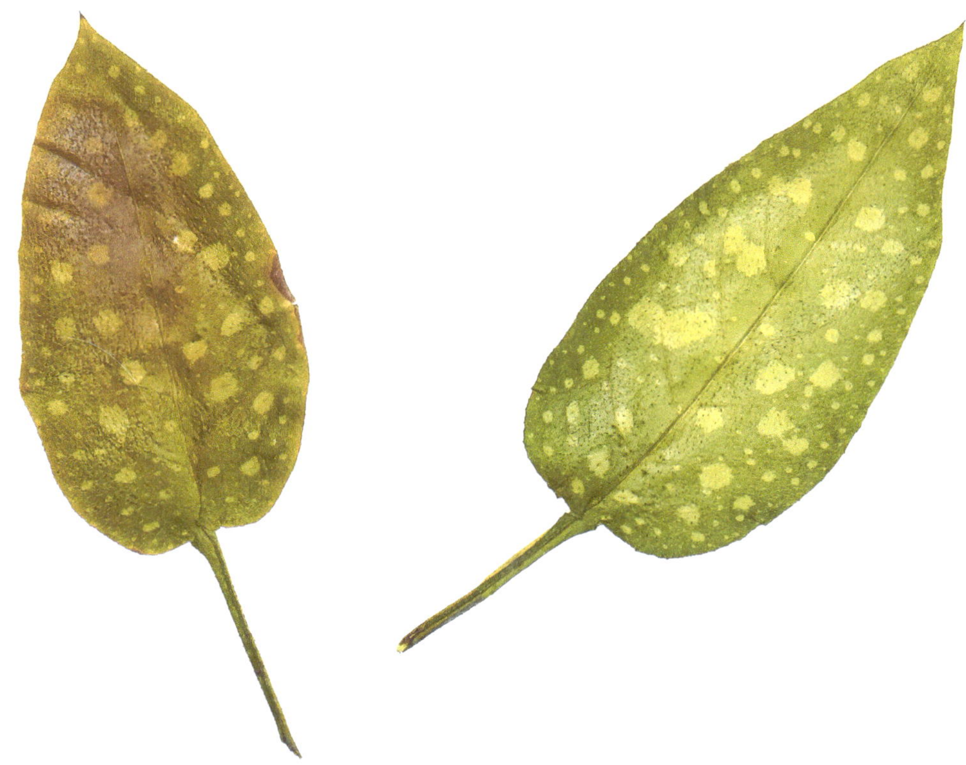

"The only way to reach these endpoints is to improve the life in the soil."

– Elaine Ingham

Dr. Ingham has become legend as the woman who defied the older men of academia who told her that fungi had no function in plant growth. She went on to establish the Soil Foodweb School and her biological approach to agriculture triggered the Soil Renaissance.

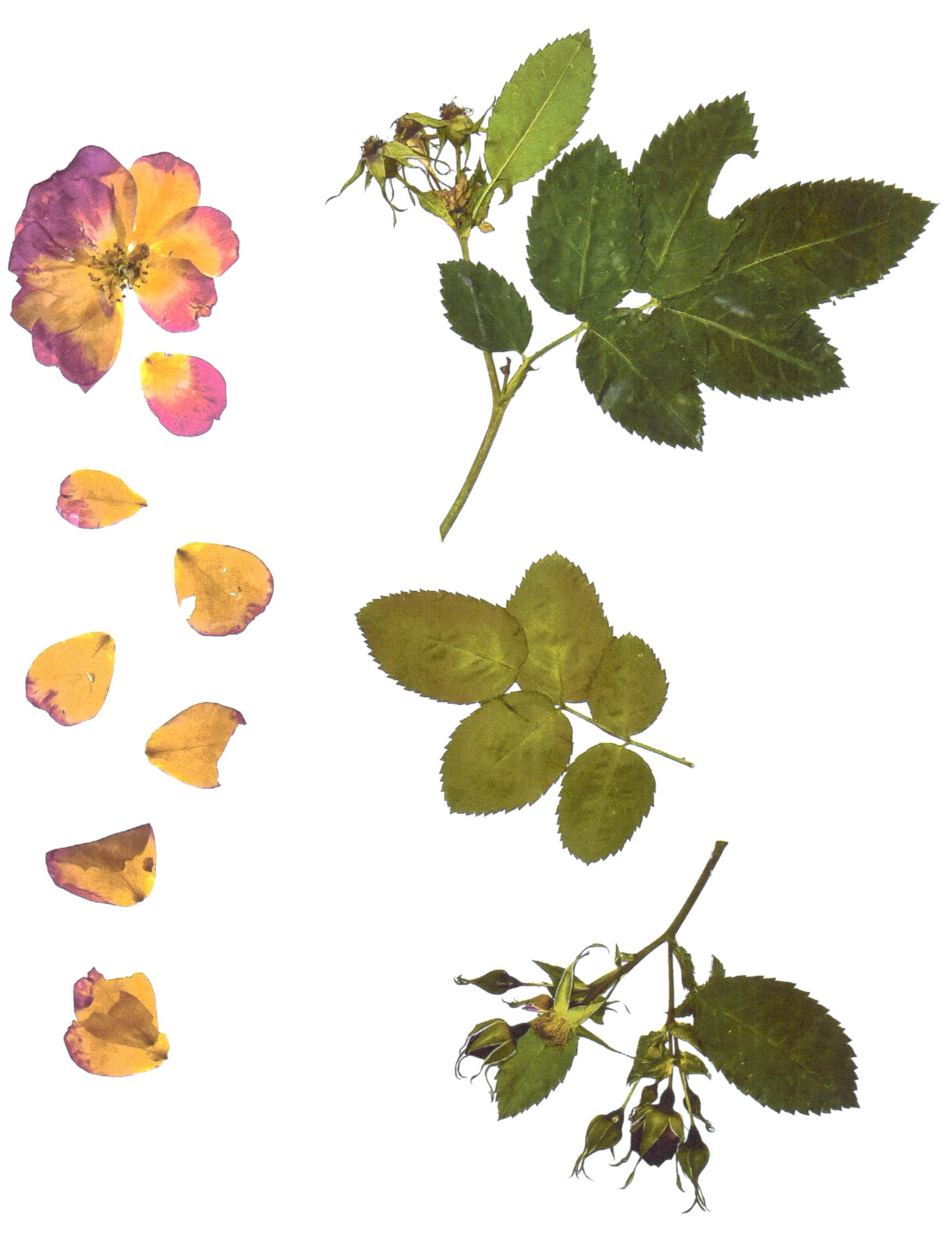

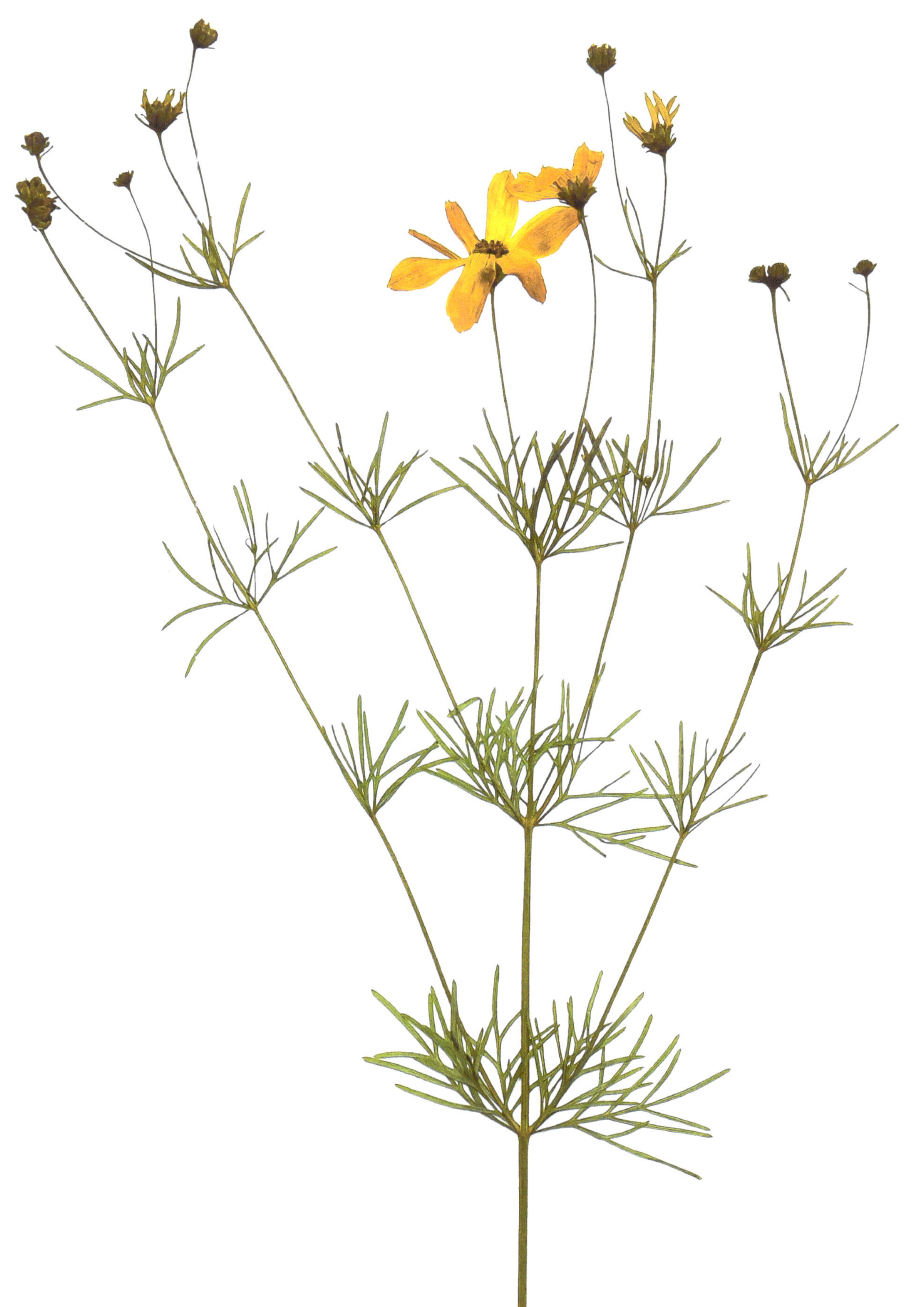

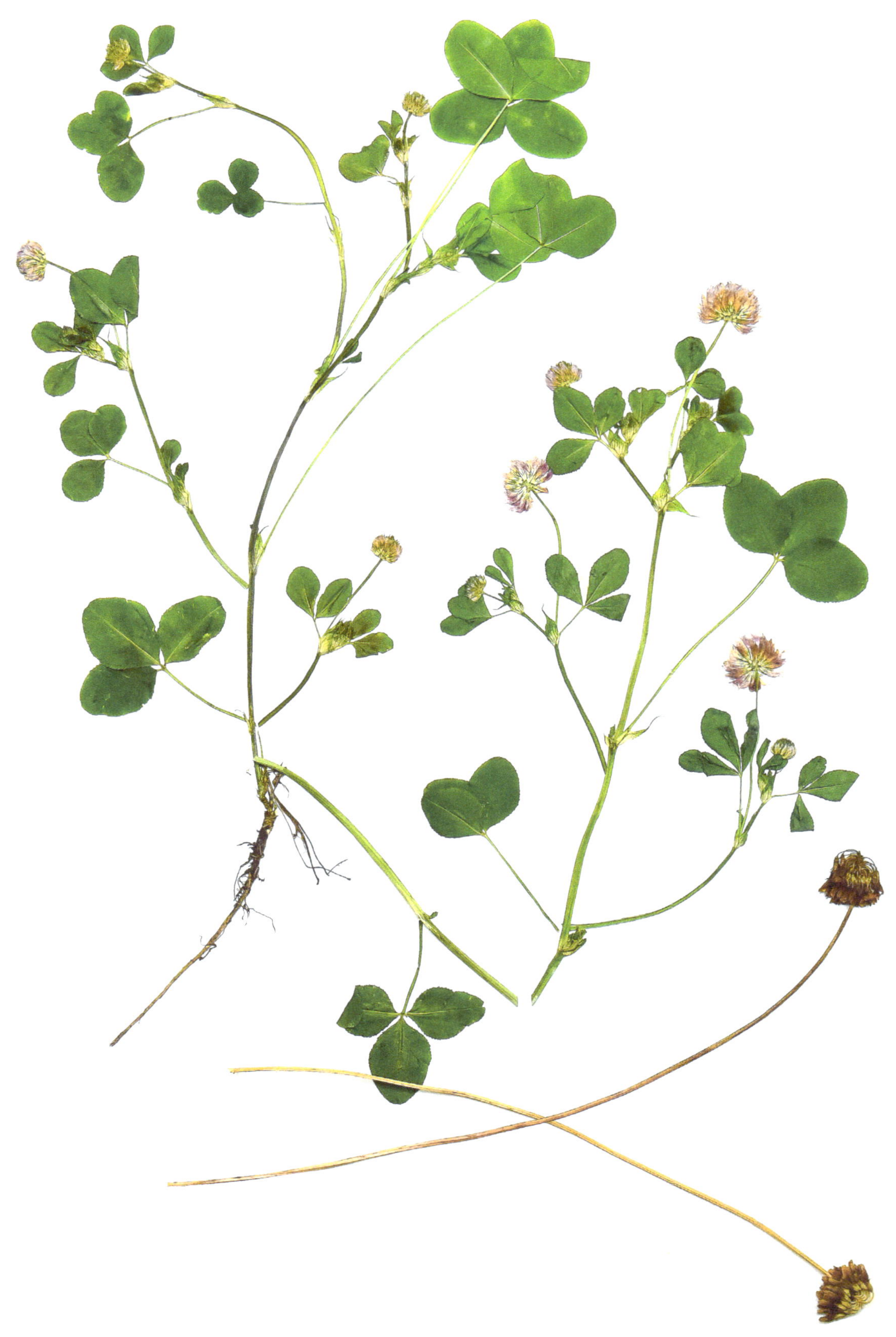

Advancing Eco Agriculture is a leader in regenerative practice and has helped numerous farmers and ranchers find greater success by growing healthier plants. A beautiful plant is not the result of building the perfect soil test, it comes from good cultural management.

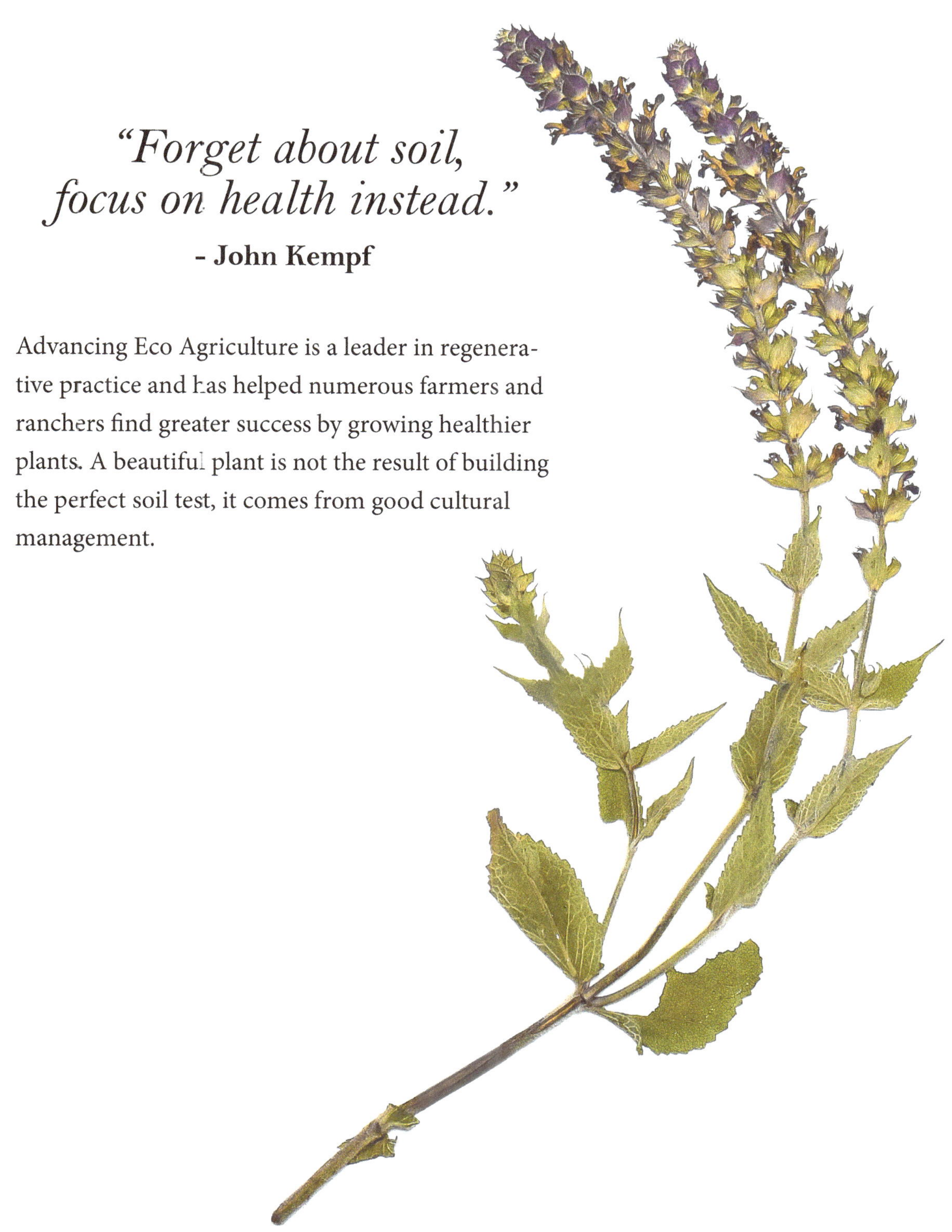

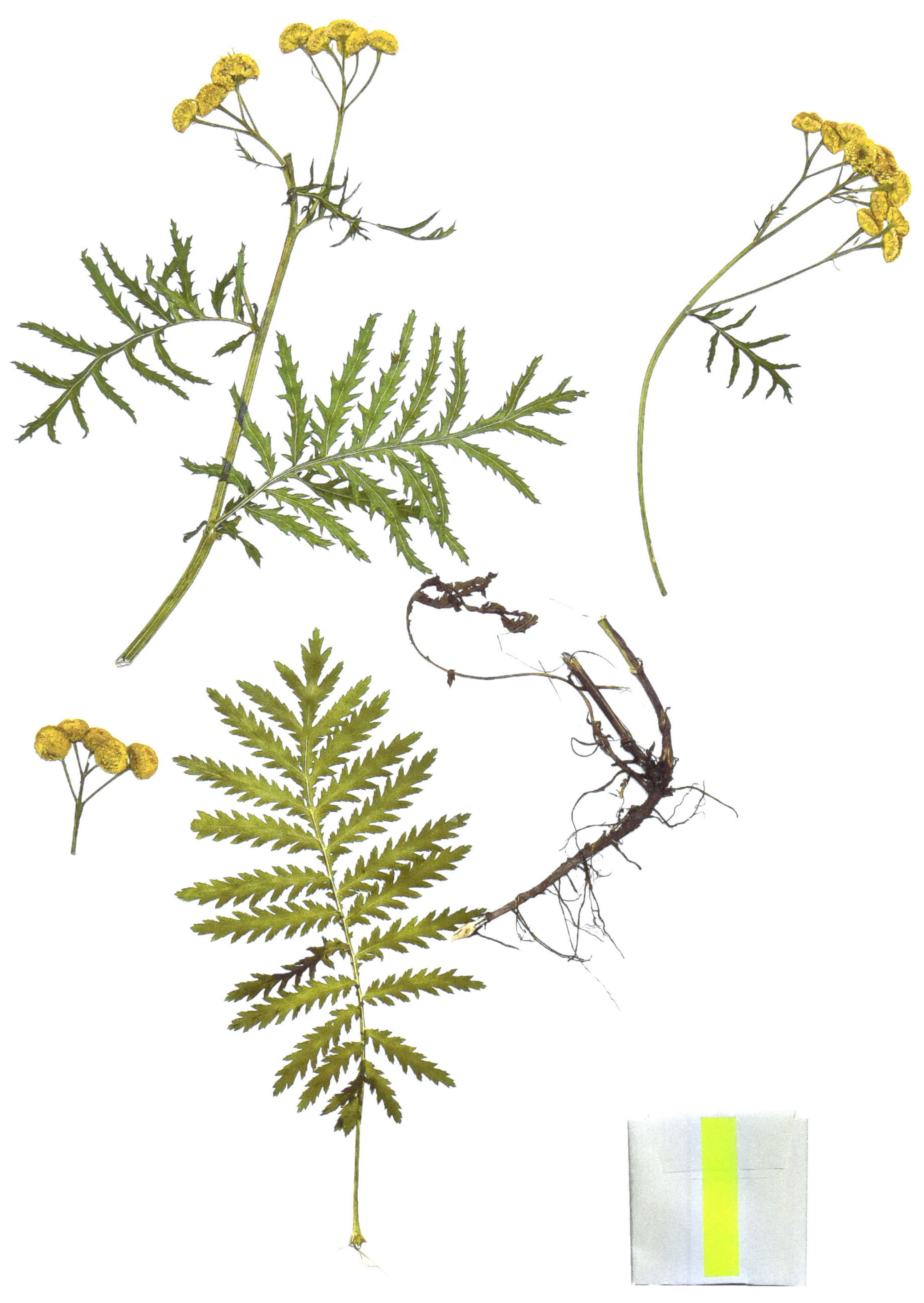

Eternal Summer

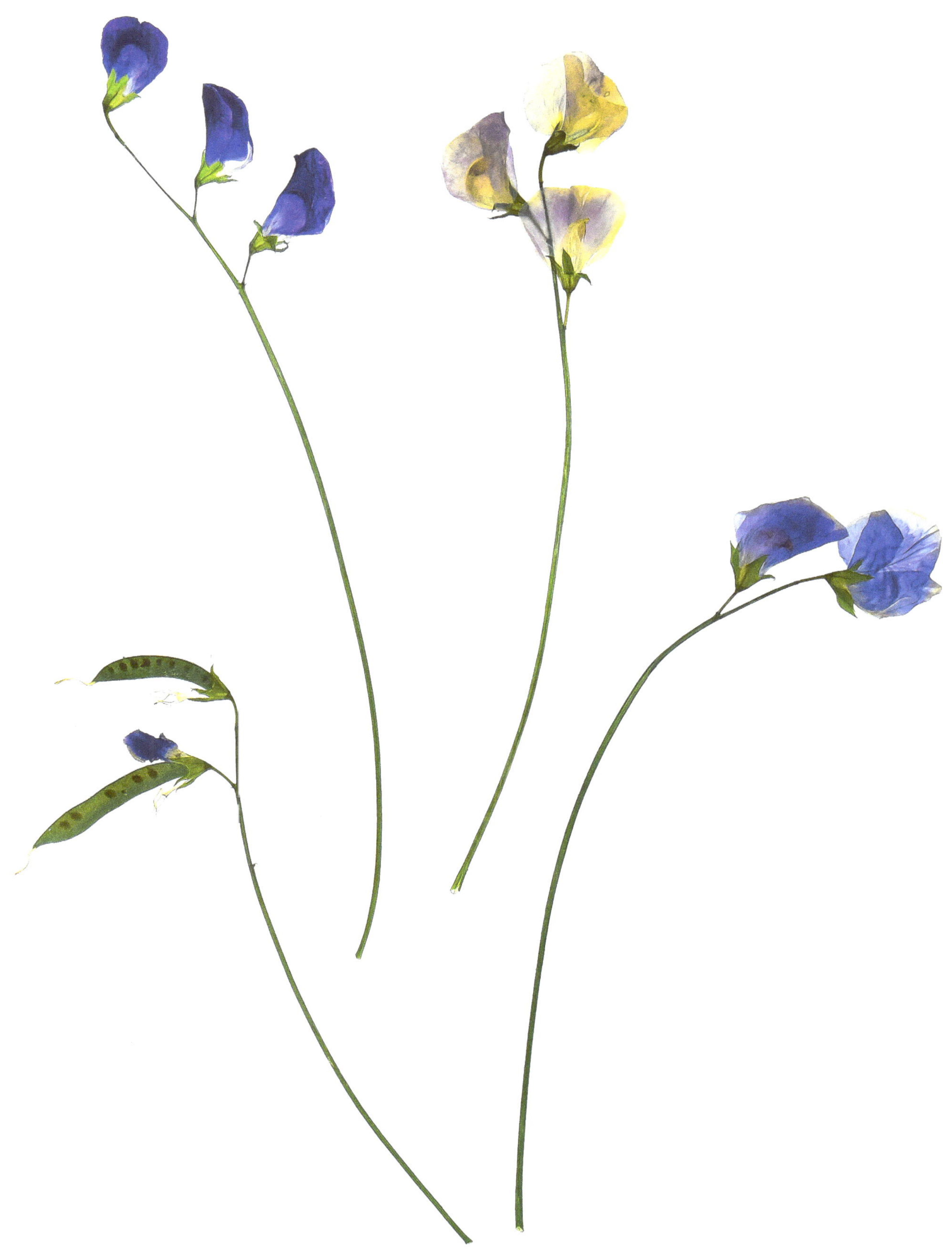

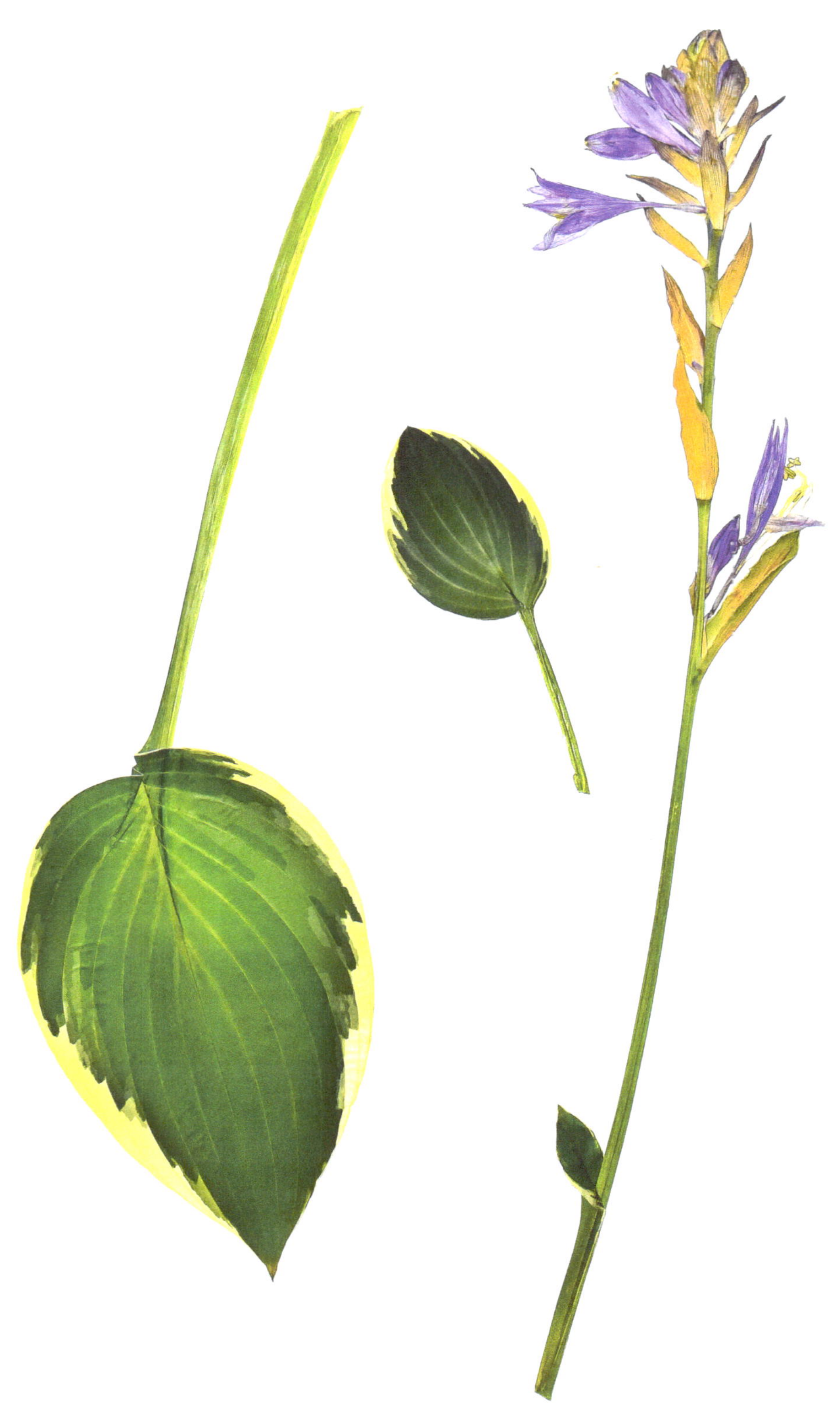

Eternal Summer

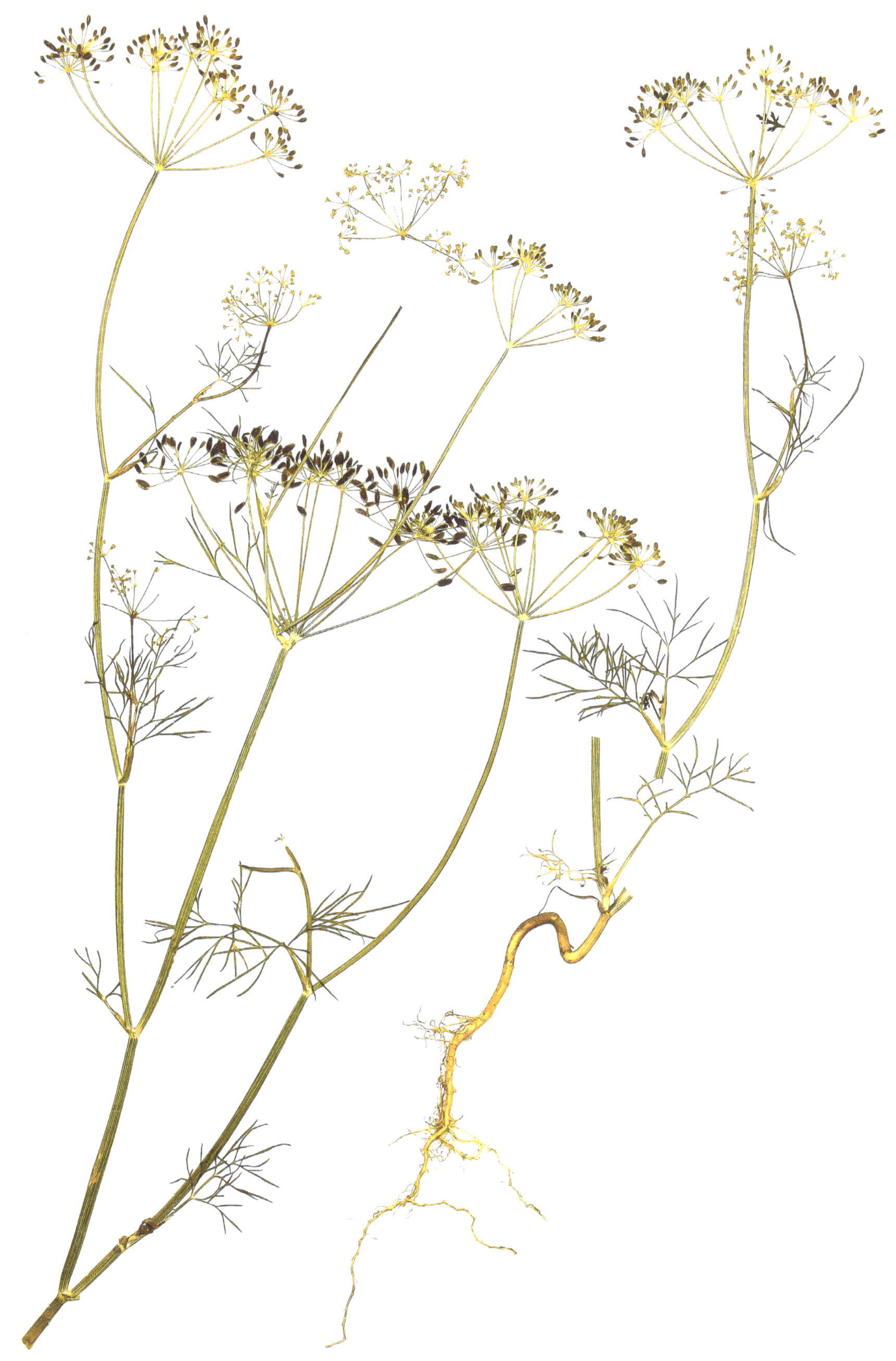

Create Your Own Plant Collection

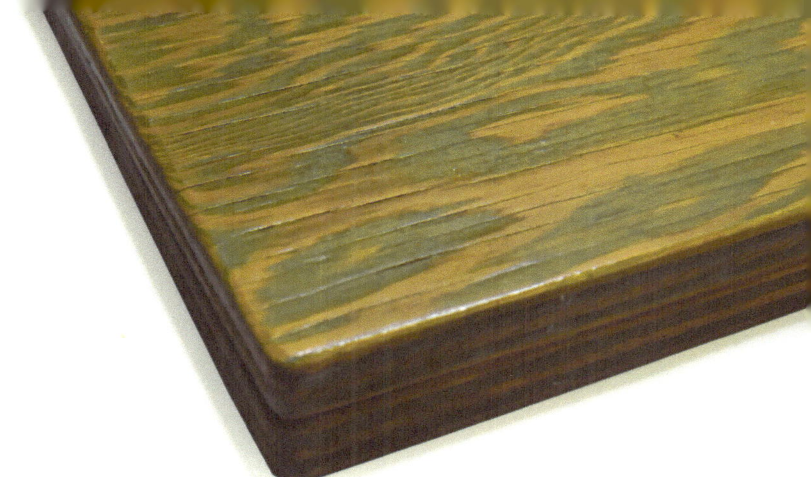

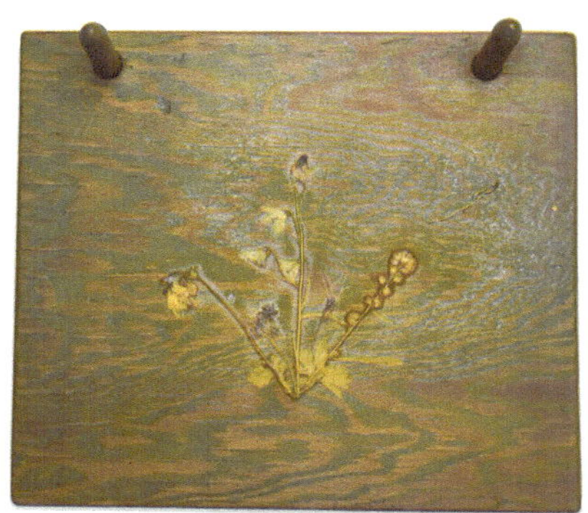

*"Look deep into nature,
and you will understand
everything better."*

– Albert Einstein

Those who value herbaria for the information they contain compare it to a library in organic form. The specimens, which may be sold or traded with other collectors, may be compared to currency in a botanical form.

There is a useful video guide by the New York Botanical Garden on YouTube titled "Herbarium at Home," and numerous others are available online through societies, governments, and universities.

Herbarium Themes

If you want your collection to have a theme, here are ideas for the budding botanist:

Plants in My Garden - The simplest way to get plant samples at the various stages you need is to have them close by. Plants are at their peak early in the morning, and harvesting them is a great way to start your day.

May Blooms - Here are some early flowers to cultivate in Alberta in the month of May: Willow, Stinkweed, Squill, Hepatica, Violet, Alexander, Bleeding Heart, Tulip, Lewisia, and Dandelion. These are the first food for our threatened pollinators.

I Love Thee Not - Creeping Thistle, Creeping Bellflower, Common Groundsel, Knotweed, Sow Thistle, Pigweed, and Smooth Brome. These plants speak to this theme as they are considered undesirable by many. As master gardeners learn to view these species through an ecological lens, the theme shifts to one of healing and of "Life's longing for itself." Quote by Kahlil Gibran.

Plants Native to Alberta - Violet, Alexander, Prairie Buttercup, Prairie Crocus, Blue Flax, Bergamot, Joe Pye, Hedysarum, Penstemon, Solidago, and Aster. These species are easy to grow in any garden and make a big contribution towards restoring our damaged ecosystems.

Biodynamic Garden - Borage, Chamomile, Comfrey, Nettle, Horsetail, Nasturtium, Yarrow, Dandelion, Valerian, and Oak. Biodynamics was one of the first Organic Gardening movements based on natural nutrient cycling. It is a holistic, ecological, and ethical approach to agriculture and nutrition.

Friendship Garden - The traditional colour of friendship is yellow. Collect and press bright, sunny flowers and create a one-of-a-kind greeting card.

Midnight Ramble - Take a stroll after dark and nab a sample of whatever plants your

neighbours have in abundance. (Just kidding! Don't
do this.)

Touchable - Artemisia, Lamb's Ears, Dusty Miller,
Liquorice Plant, Fountain Grass, Irish Moss,
Mullein, and Pussy Willow. These plants have
soft-textured leaves and blooms.

Fascinating Foliage - Fern, Oak, Cut-Leaf Birch,
Hosta, Opuntia, Begonia, Prayer Plant, Curly Endive,
Radicchio, Giant Waterlily . Unusually shaped leaves
add drama to your collection. (Giant waterlily is a
botanical joke and shouldn't be attempted because
the leaves are a metre across and 2-3 cm thick!)

Rhythmic - Plants named in song titles. Think
"Orange Blossom Special" by Johnny Cash, "Passion-
fruit" by Drake, or "Edelweiss" by Julie Andrews. A
hundred other titles come up in a Google search, but
"Dead Flowers" by The Rolling Stones works for
any.

Bridal Bouquet - What was in your bouquet, and
why did you choose it? Perhaps your wedding flowers will take on new meanings for you after this
project.

Go Away! - Stinging Nettle, Garlic, Hoya, Buffa-
loberry, Castor Bean, Poison Ivy, Monkshood, and
Corpse Flower. These plants smell bad or can cause
harm or even death. (Again, just kidding. You've been
warned!)

What I did on my Summer Vacation - A trav-
el-themed collection of plants from the places you
have visited near and far.

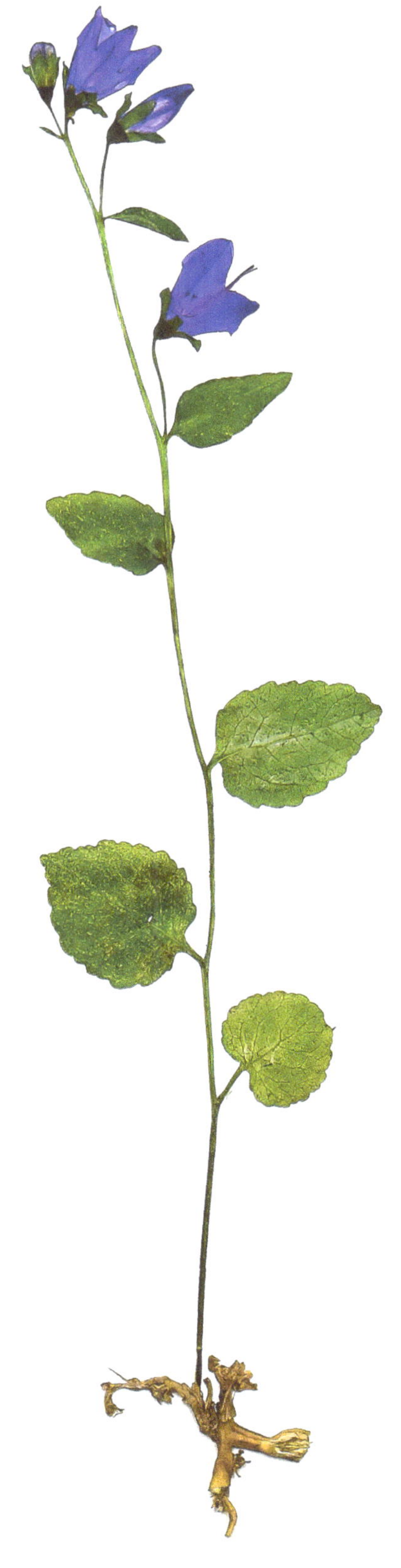

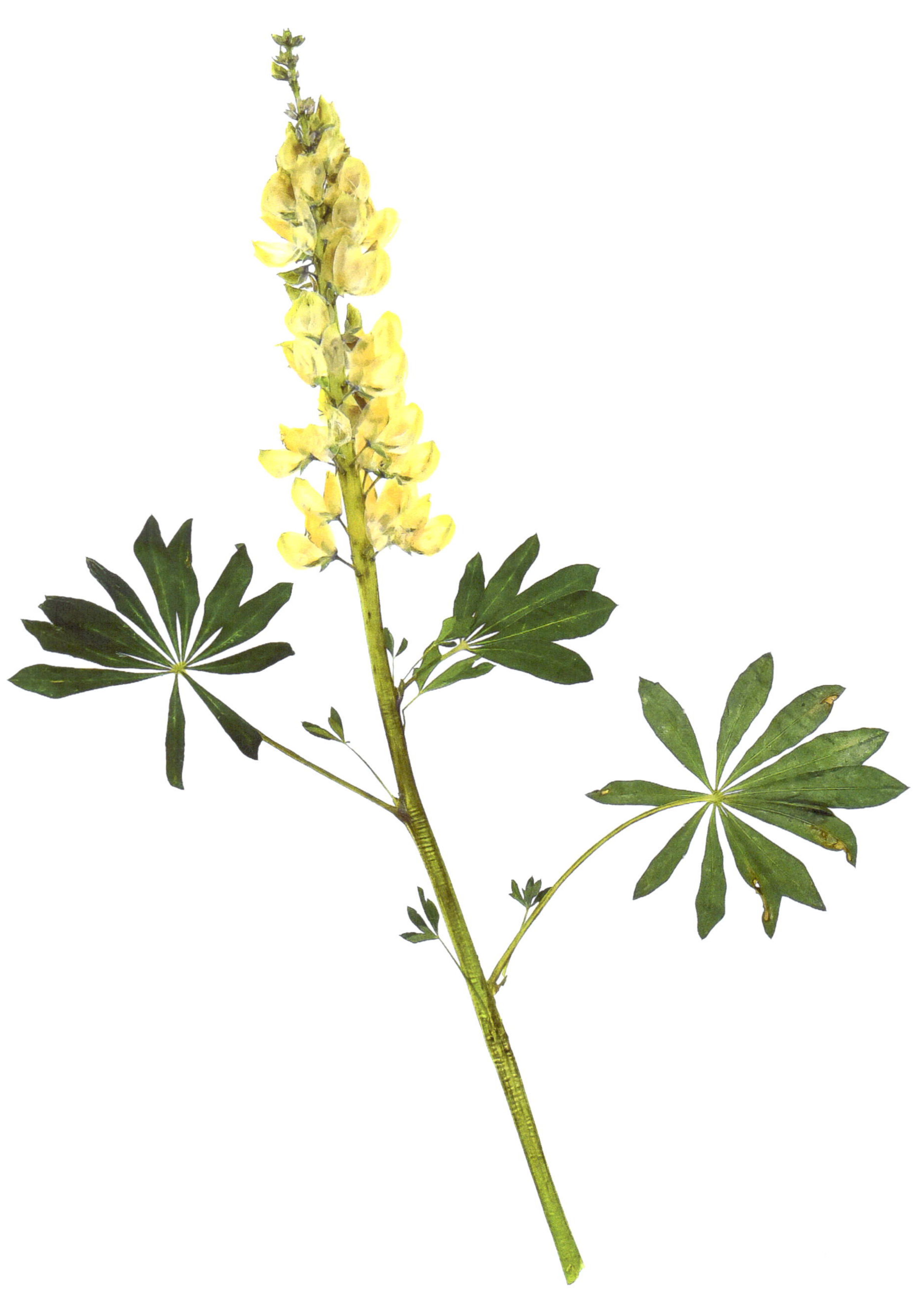

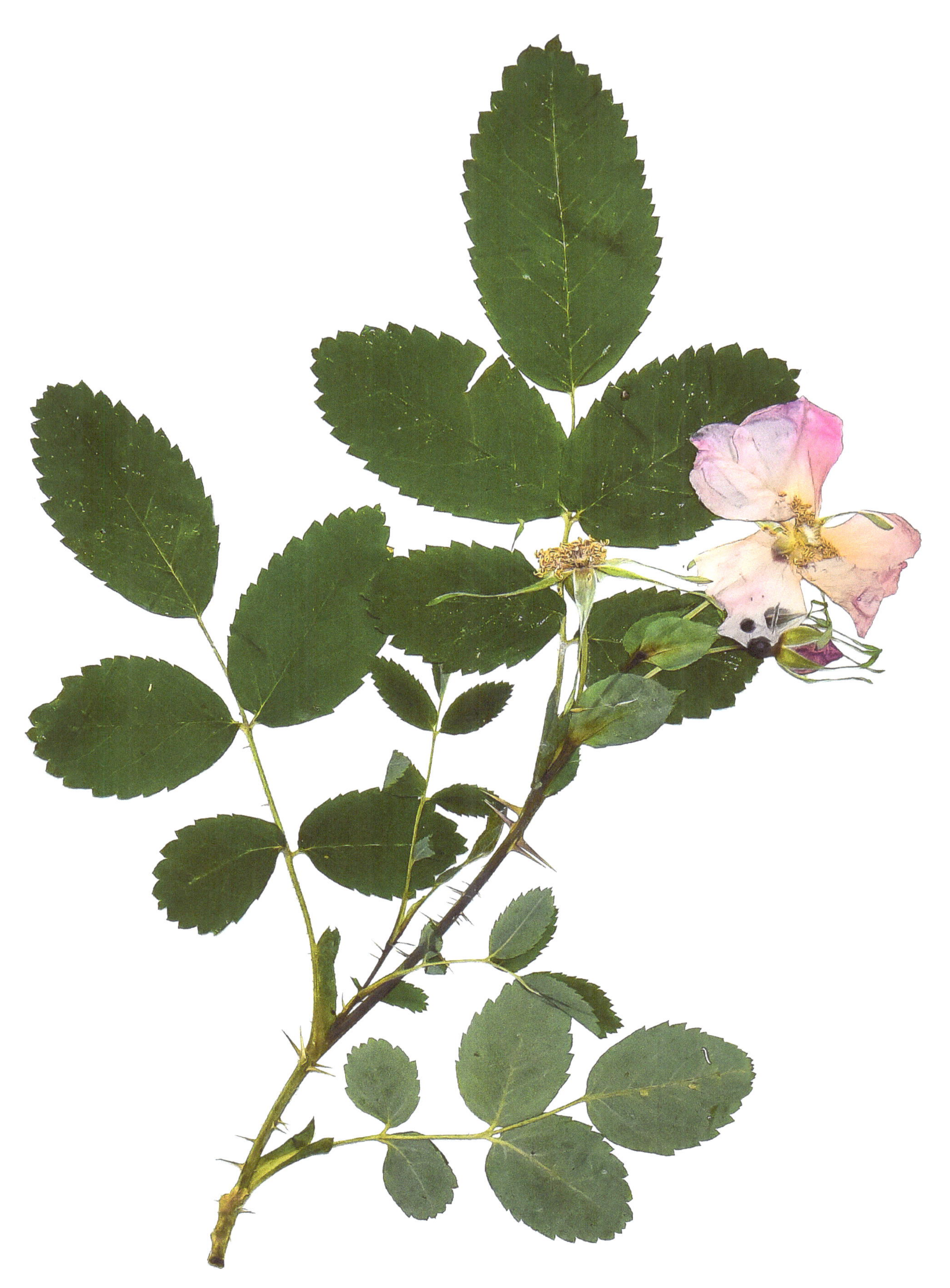

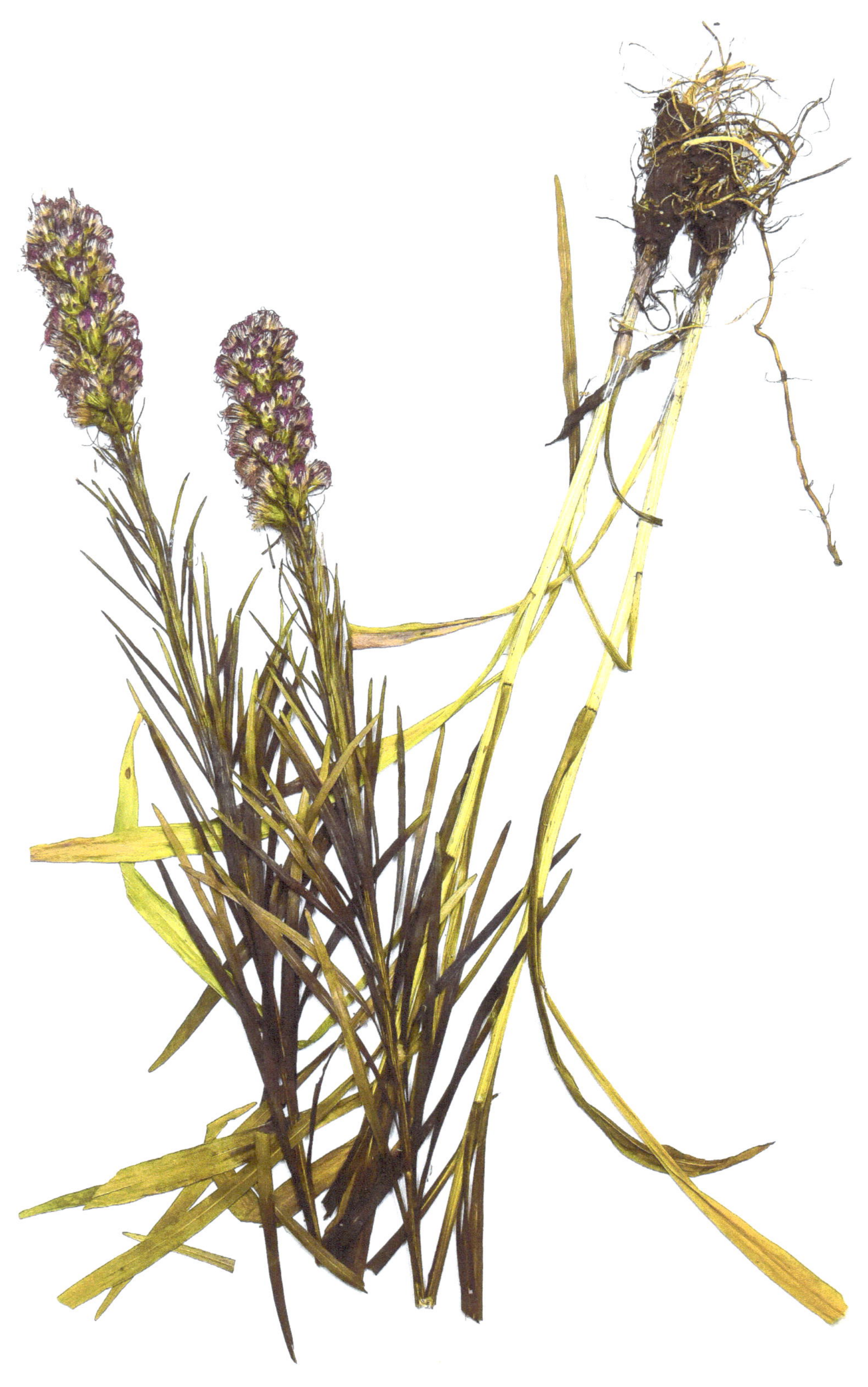

Eternal Summer

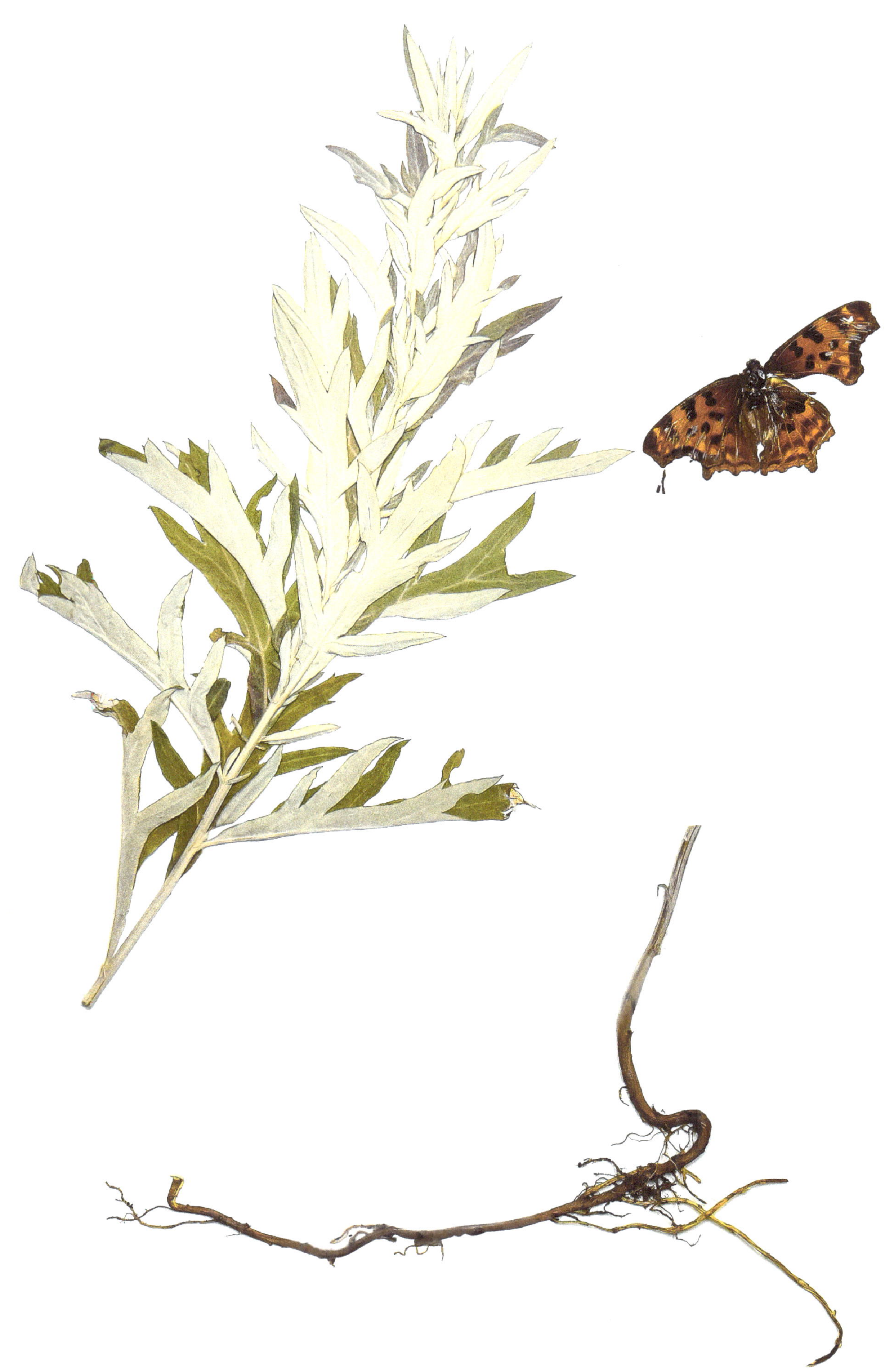

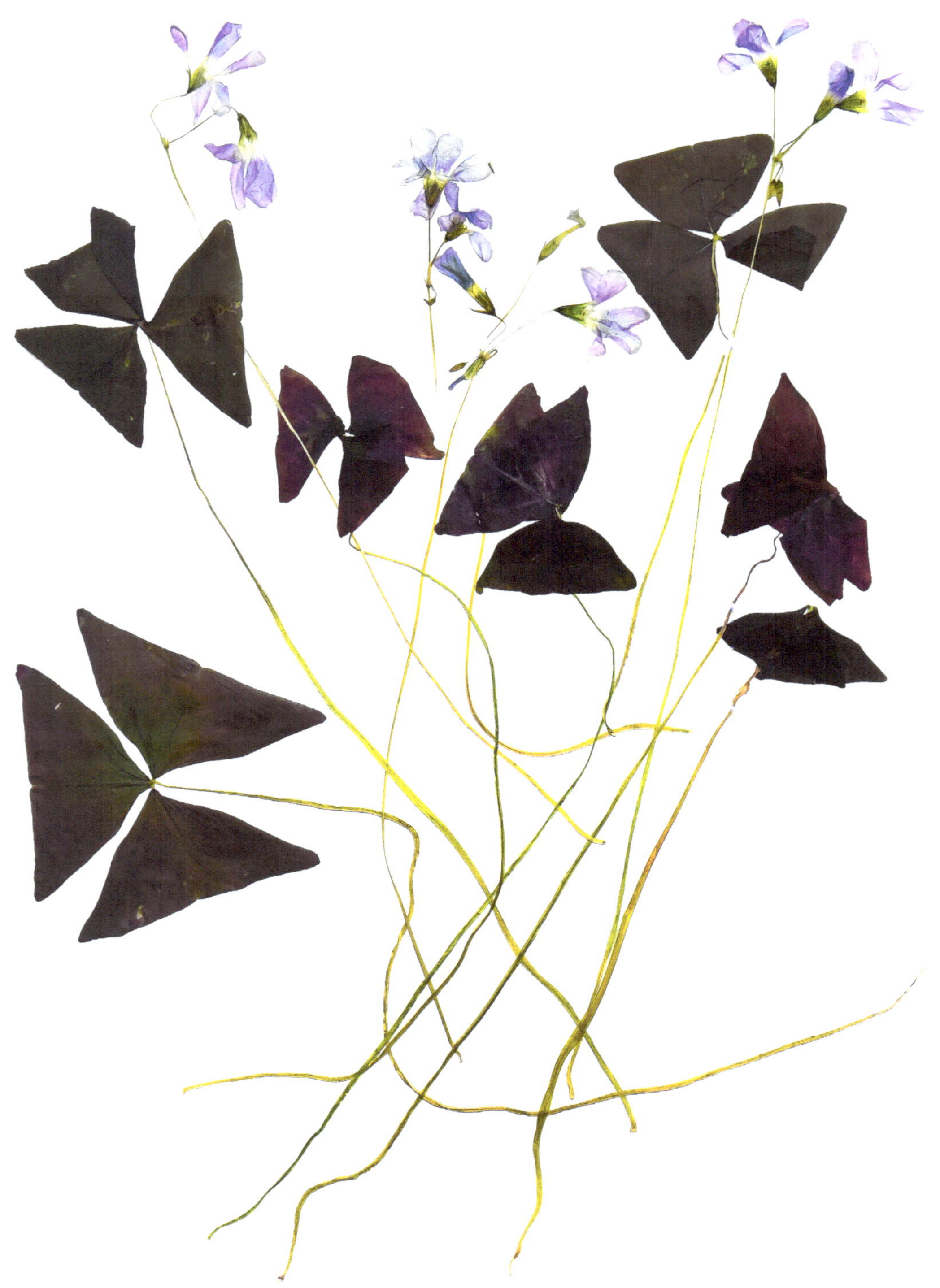

Eternal Summer

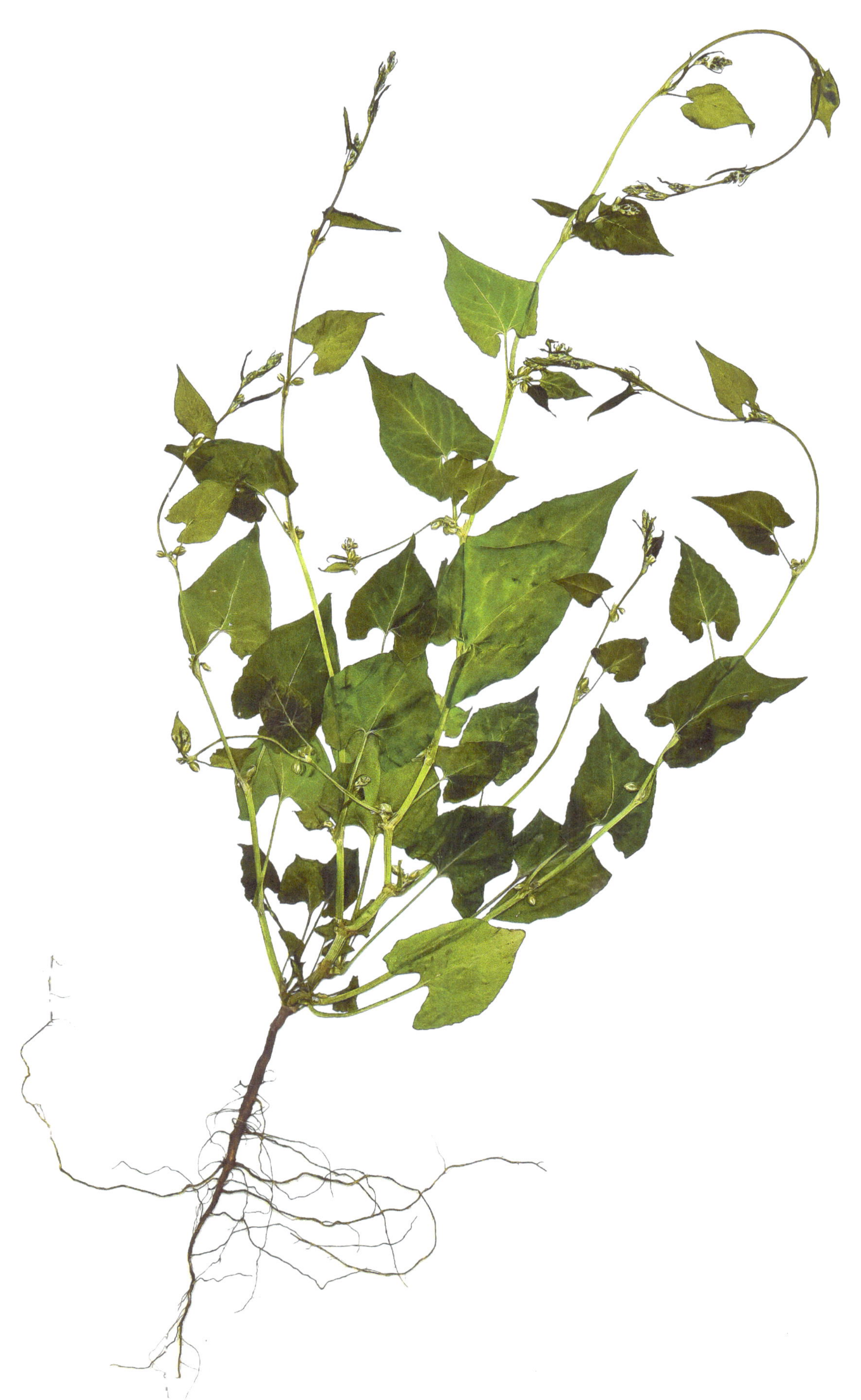

"Mulch, Moisture, and Microbes."
- Heidi Hermary

You don't get much simpler than Heidi's 3M approach to gardening—keep the soil covered, don't let the soil get too dry or too wet, and use photosynthesis and compost to increase biodiversity.

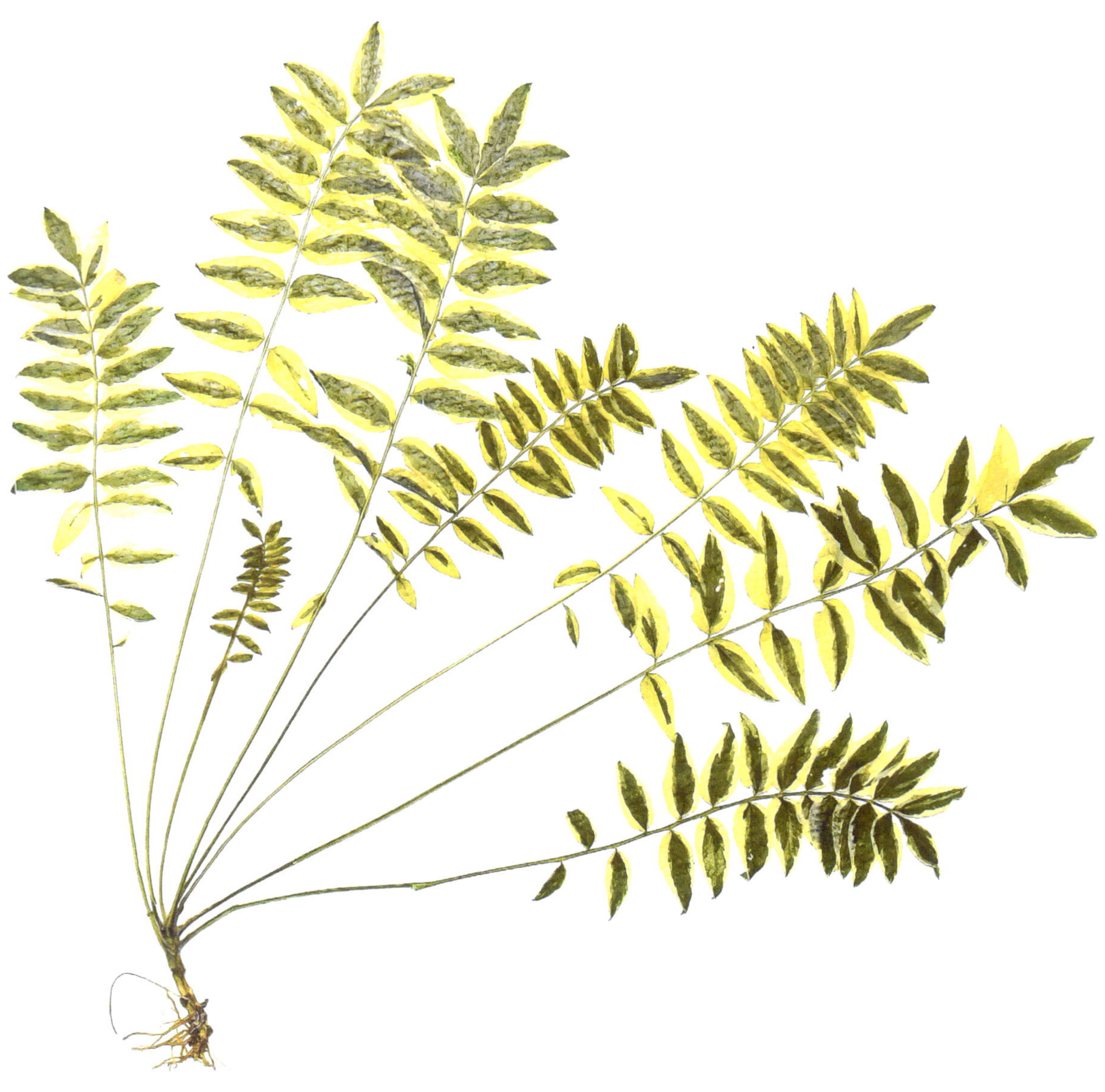

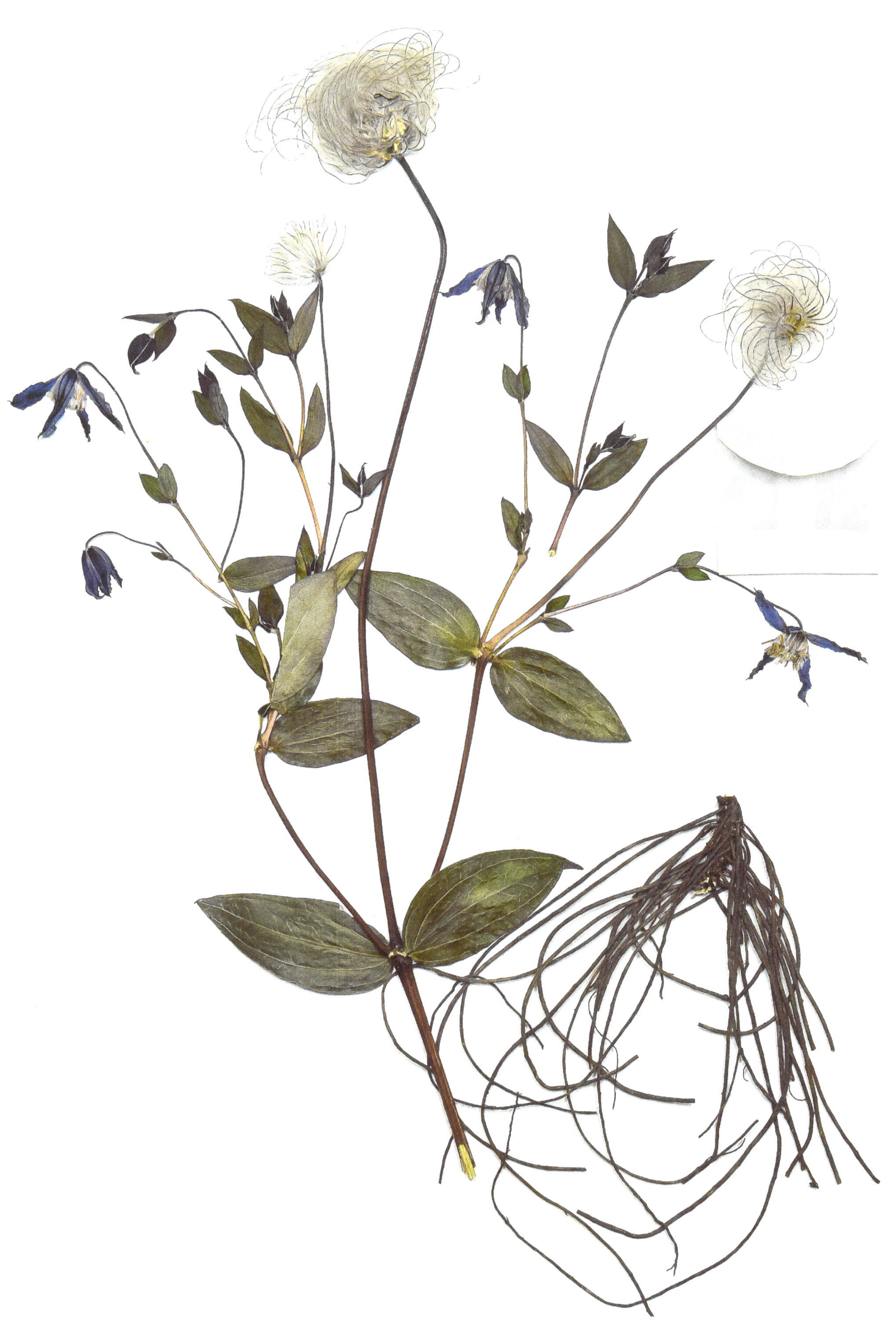

Alberta Person of Interest: George Pegg

As an amateur botanist, George Pegg collected plant specimens on his property, in the surrounding neighbourhood, and at several places in north-central Alberta. Once collected and pressed, George used his extensive library of botanical books to identify the specimens. For each plant, George collected several samples. Looking through his correspondence, we know George worked with botanists from several agencies, mailing them specimens for verification of his identification. While George kept his own sample, the ones he mailed became part of their collection.

After he died in 1988, his family donated more than 3,000 of George's pressed plants to the Royal Alberta Museum [RAM]. Each summer, the RAM loans several of his herbarium specimens for display at the George Pegg Botanic Garden. On the RAM specimens, we can see George's handwritten notes, each with a collection number he used to track his work. The specimens have a historical significance. Because they record the place where the plants were collected, we can see when and where George travelled.

It is because of George Pegg's botanical work that the Pegg homestead is a designated provincial Historic Resource. The display of herbarium specimens is a tangible way to help visitors understand the work he did. These specimens are the way our site interpreters start the story of the significance of herbarium collections across the world. Our visitors often take a close look at the fine details of the pressed plants, comment on the surprisingly vibrant colours of some samples, and are delighted to see some of the same plants blooming in the Garden on the day of their visit.

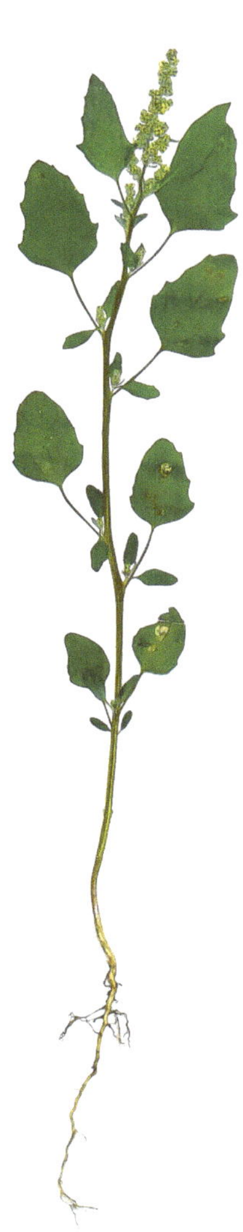

Source: George Pegg Botanic Garden Society. The Garden is located at 56015 Range Road 43, Lac Ste. Anne County, 2.5 km North of Highway 43, Glenevis, Alberta. Website: www.pegggarden.org

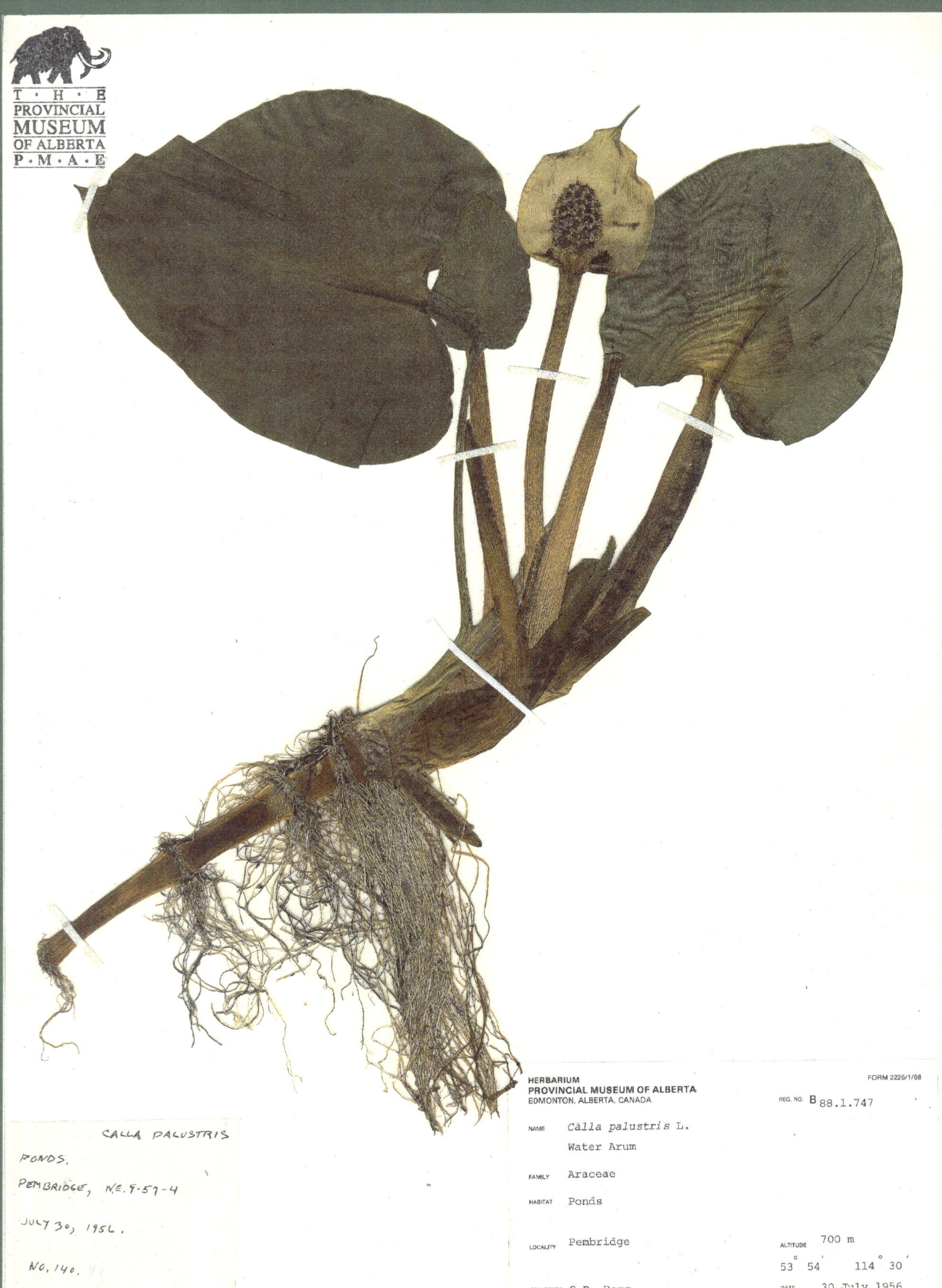

T·H·E
PROVINCIAL
MUSEUM
OF ALBERTA
P·M·A·E

CALLA PALUSTRIS
PONDS.
PEMBRIDGE, N.E.9-57-4
JULY 30, 1956.
NO.140.
WATER ARUM

HERBARIUM
PROVINCIAL MUSEUM OF ALBERTA
EDMONTON, ALBERTA, CANADA
FORM 2226/1/88
REG. NO. B 88.1.747
NAME   Calla palustris L.
        Water Arum
FAMILY Araceae
HABITAT Ponds
LOCALITY Pembridge
ALTITUDE 700 m
53° 54'   114° 30'
COLLECTOR G.R. Pegg
DATE 30 July 1956
DET BY G.R.P.
CONFIRMED

The Botanist

George Robert Pegg is one of Alberta's most extraordinary historical figures. He has left an indelible mark, not only on the local lives in the community of Lac St. Anne but on the botanical and scientific communities as well.

George was a self-taught botanist with a discerning "eye" that detected even the most subtle differences in plant variation. The plants that George collected and studied were primarily those that were native to our province. He meticulously pressed them in plant presses and documented their collection and distributional data contributing to our present understanding of Alberta's diverse flora. He discovered many "first records" of plant species in Alberta and his contributions to E.H. Moss' notable "Flora of Alberta" are well recognized in the scientific community.

Through his specimens, and their associated data, George also provided us, unknowingly, with a valuable historical record of the changes that have occurred in our biodiversity from the time of collection to the present. This knowledge continues to assist current conservation and biodiversity initiatives.

Herbarium Specimens

After the passing of George, in 1988, the Pegg family donated his collection of pressed plants to the Royal Alberta Museum Herbarium (a library of dried plant specimens). The Pegg Collection, comprised of approximately 4000 specimens, included vascular plants, mosses, lichens, and liverworts.

The vascular plants were received in folded sheets of newspaper, with a small hand-written label, made by George. The staff at the Museum mounted the plants onto herbarium sheets and created a Museum label from the information George provided.

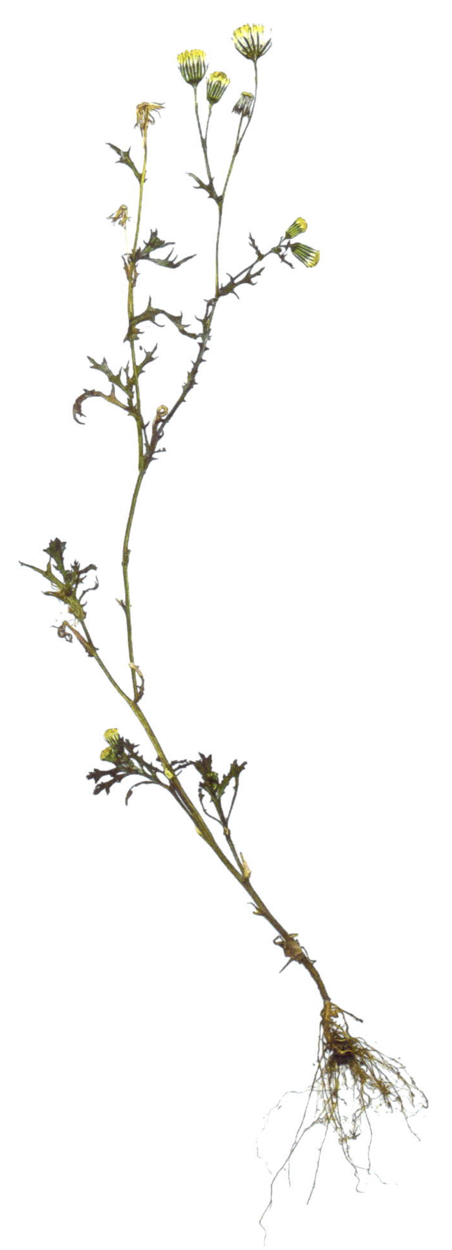

His original label was retained and mounted onto the sheet. After processing, the Pegg Collection was integrated into the Museum's herbarium and database, thereby making this noteworthy collection accessible to the general public and scientific community.

George also had a fascination with gardening. He created his own garden by planting exotic seeds and seedlings from all over the world as well as transplanting native plants from other regions of Alberta. Some of the specimens he collected from his garden are part of the collection given to the Museum.

The superb plant preservation and pressing techniques of George's specimens, as well as the Garden itself, offer evidence of the dedication and passion he expressed throughout his life.

Source: George Pegg display information written by Donna Cherniawsky, Assistant Curator of Botany. Royal Alberta Museum Herbarium

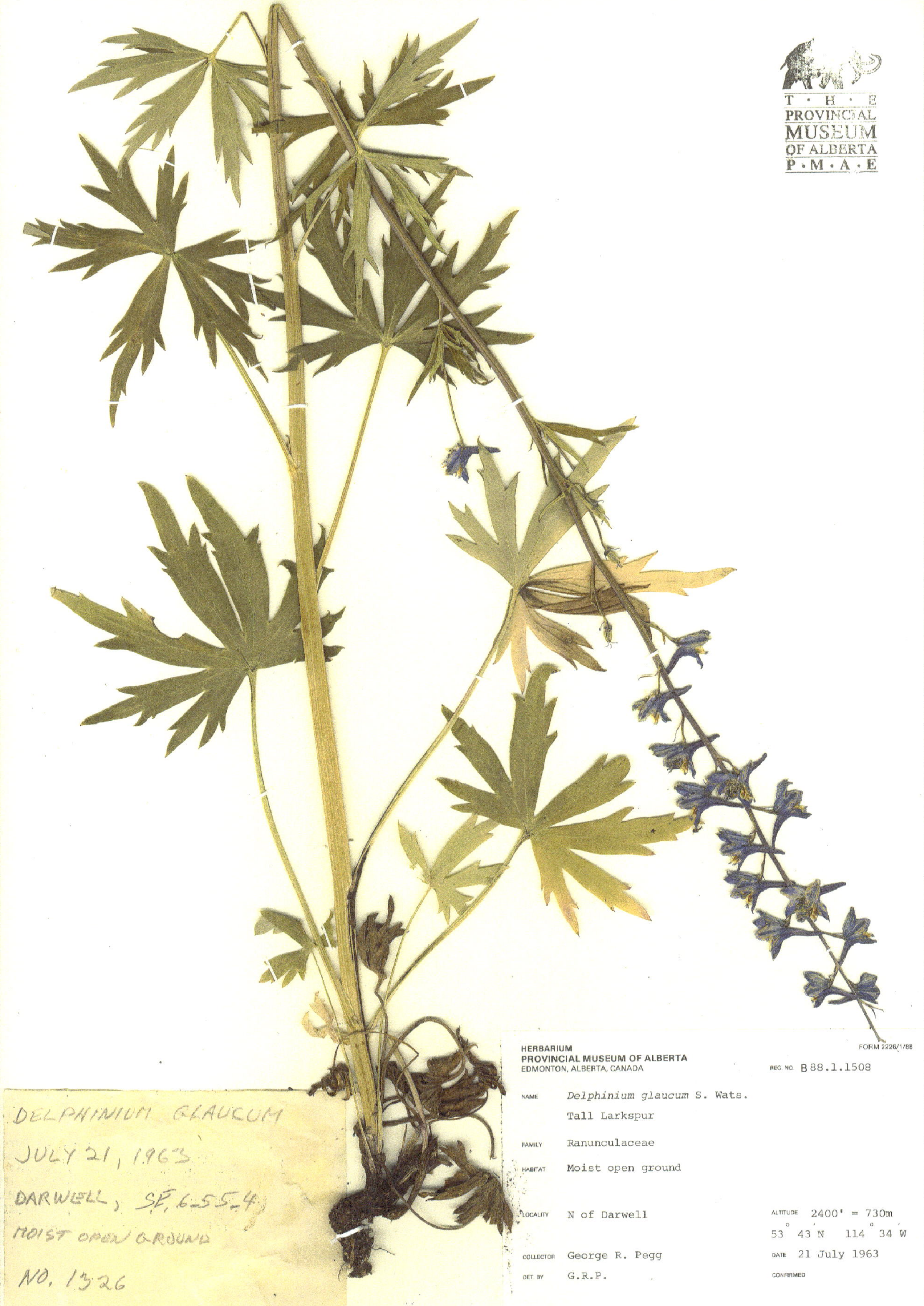

DELPHINIUM GLAUCUM
JULY 21, 1963
DARWELL, S.E. 6-55-4
MOIST OPEN GROUND
NO. 1326
THE PROVINCIAL MUSEUM OF ALBERTA P·M·A·E
FORM 2226/1/88
HERBARIUM
PROVINCIAL MUSEUM OF ALBERTA
EDMONTON, ALBERTA, CANADA
REG. NO. B 88.1.1508
NAME Delphinium glaucum S. Wats.
Tall Larkspur
FAMILY Ranunculaceae
HABITAT Moist open ground
LOCALITY N of Darwell
ALTITUDE 2400' = 730m
53° 43' N 114° 34' W
COLLECTOR George R. Pegg
DATE 21 July 1963
DET BY G.R.P.
CONFIRMED

Below is an Interview with George Pegg, Courtesy of the Provincial Archives of Alberta, December 29, 1979. The interview was conducted by Reevan Dolgoy of the Alberta Historical Resources Foundation. Supplied by Lorraine Taylor, Horticulturist, Lac Ste. Anne County, via Lauren Mclean, Government Records & Reference Archivist.

The following is taken from the interview introductory notes and verbatim from a transcript of the interview:

"In 1979 Reevan Dolgoy conducted an interview with George Pegg. He was with the Alberta Historical Resources Foundation at the time. Dolgoy was especially impressed with how a gifted amateur could lead the way in certain areas of botanical discovery in the province, especially in the Swan Hills area."

George Pegg: In the later years I got more interested in plants. That started because I was a farmer, and I was very fussy about weeds. I wanted to keep the farm clean so I had to identify the weeds I found, and that developed into identifying all plants…
I used to send some specimens to the university if I knew they were interested.
If it was unusual, I sent specimen[s] into the Herbarium.
Swan Hills was an interesting area because it had been visited very little. There were some interesting plants there.

Reevan Dolgoy: Why was it so interesting?

George Pegg: Well, there was some boreal life there. Boreal plants are normally found much farther north. It was a kind of outlier from the Rocky Mountains.

Reevan Dolgoy: Were you the first one to make these discoveries?

George Pegg: Pretty near, I think. There were no roads in there you see.
One interesting one that I found when [Dr. Ezra Moss] Moss was with me was a flower belonging to the lily family. I don't know the English name for it. It's very rare. It had never been found in Alberta. In fact I don't know if it could be found in Canada.

Reevan Dolgoy: What's it called?

George Pegg: Streptopus

Note: Streptopus [The only species in this genus in the Flora of Alberta, 1974 is S. amplexifolius.]

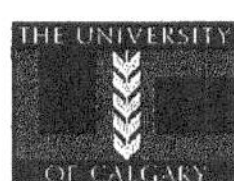

THE UNIVERSITY OF CALGARY

FACULTY OF ARTS AND SCIENCE / DEPARTMENT OF BIOLOGY

March 17, 1968

George Pegg
Glenevis, Alberta

Dear George:

Under separate cover I have just sent my revised flora of the Alberta Sphagna and Musci. I think that you will find it a real improvement over the previous one. If you find any bugs in it I would appreciate learning of them.

I enclose the determinations or verifications of the remainder of the specimens that you sent down. I must say that it has been a very interesting lot and that I have been really impressed with your ability to pick up good things. Your skill at determination is very good as well.

This last lot contains a number of noteworthy items. The Discelium nudum is most interesting. I though that you must be wrong to begin with as all previous North American collections have been from the northeastern United States. There seems no doubt, however, that you are correct. The $64 question is how it managed to get to the Swan Hills. Three other species, Mnium andrewsianum, Pogonatum urnigerum and Mielichhoferia macrocarpa, are all second records for Alberta. The latter was described on the basis of material collected in the Jasper Park area by Thomas Drummond, the first person to collect bryophytes in the province. I plan to mention all of the four except the Pogonatum in the paper that I mentioned in my last letter.

Sincerely,

C. D. Bird

P.S. You are quite correct that several of your lichens are unreported for Alberta. I do have other specimens of these, however. I have so many unreported lichens that I am not quite certain how to handle them. A simple additions paper does not seem quite right.

THE UNIVERSITY OF CALGARY / CALGARY, ALBERTA, CANADA / AREA CODE 403. TELEPHONE 282-0110

George Pegg corresponded with many agencies across Canada. These historical letters, ranging from 1968 to 1988, demonstrate the valuable contribution of George's specimens. The letter writers encourage George to continue his work.

UNIVERSITY OF SASKATCHEWAN

SASKATOON, CANADA

April 29, 1969

Mr. George Pegg
Glenevis, Alberta

Dear Mr. Pegg:

I have looked over your very interesting willow collection from last summer. For the most part they were correctly identified and I have made only a few changes.

The specimens that were correctly identified are:

2965   *S. sitchensis*
3045   *S. glauca*
3047   *S. barrattiana*
2990   *S. pedicellaris*
2992   *S. maccalliana*
2991   *S. candida*
2989   *S. pyrifolia*
2994   *S. myrtillifolia*
3021   *S. vestita*
2987   *S. athabascensis*
3019   *S. farrae*

The name that I am using for <u>Salix farrae</u> is <u>S. hastata</u> L. This change was made by Hultén in his latest flora of Alaska and I agreed with him.

Numbers 9282 and 9283 are <u>Salix alba</u> L. This is a commonly cultivated willow in central North America. Specimen number 2984 is the tall form of <u>Salix myrtillifolia</u> which I am calling <u>Salix novae-angliae</u>. I am discussing my reasons for choosing this name in a treatment of the <u>Salix</u> of Alaska and Yukon which has been completed and is now looking for a publisher.

Specimens 2993 and 3058 seem to represent a hybrid of some kind but it looks more like a <u>Salix</u> <u>commutata</u> or a <u>Salix</u> <u>candida</u> than <u>Salix</u> <u>athabascensis</u> × <u>pedicellaris</u>. Does <u>Salix</u> <u>commutata</u> occur in the area in which this hybrid was found? There are no collections of this species in the plants you sent to me but it is to be expected in the Rocky Mountains.

. . . 2

Mr. George Pegg   -2-   April 29, 1969

     I will be leaving for a new position at the Museum of
Natural History, University of Oregon, Eugene, Oregon, the end
of this summer. I will be continuing my work on _Salix_ and I
would like to have you continue sending me specimens for
identification.

                              Sincerely yours,

                              George W. Argus

GWA:lh

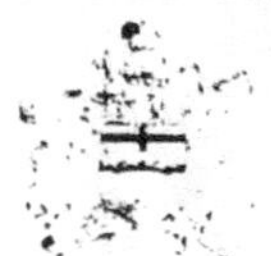

CULTURE

103 Legislature Building. Edmonton. Alberta. Canada T5K 2B6   403/427-4928

March 14, 1988

Mr. Harry Pegg
8934 - 94 Avenue
Edmonton, Alberta
T6C 1W7

Dear Mr. Pegg:

It has come to my attention that you were instrumental in donating to the people of Alberta, via the Botany Program at the Provincial Museum, the highly valued collection of plant specimens, records, papers, books, journals and other periodicals that had belonged to your late brother, Mr. George Pegg. On behalf of Alberta Culture and Multiculturalism, I would like to thank you, and other members of the family, for this generous and greatly appreciated donation. Also at this time I would like to offer my condolences to you and to other members of the family on the passing of your brother George.

Your brother was well known and highly regarded in natural history, especially botanical circles, for his thorough and meticulous work and his attention to detail. His plant collections, which are now deposited in the Provincial Museum herbarium, are important for several reasons. I understand that some of them are the first Alberta records of several species. Also, the musum has had few plant specimens from the areas in which your brother made his collections and documentations. Thus, your brother's specimens will now supplement and fill in the gaps in the museum collections, and will thereby greatly increase the usefulness of the Provincial Museum herbarium in studies of Alberta vegetation by the staff, other botanists, students and other interested members of the public. Your brother's highly regarded work will therefore be continued, and appreciated, into the future.

Again, I thank you for your thoughtfulness in donating the very valuable plant collections, and other materials, that are a truly significant addition to the heritage of our province.

Yours truly,

Greg Stevens, P.Eng.
Minister of Alberta Culture
  and Multiculturalism

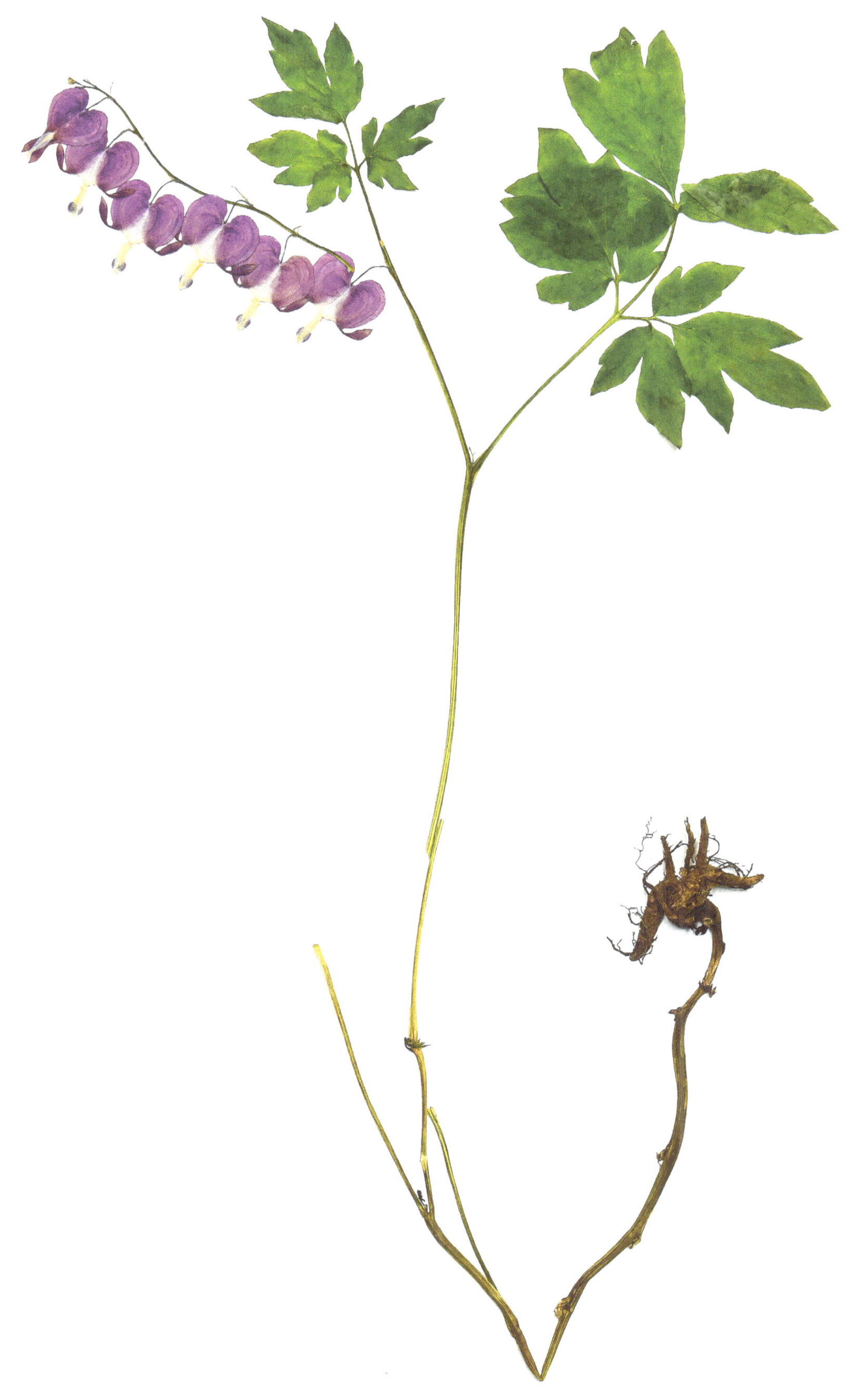

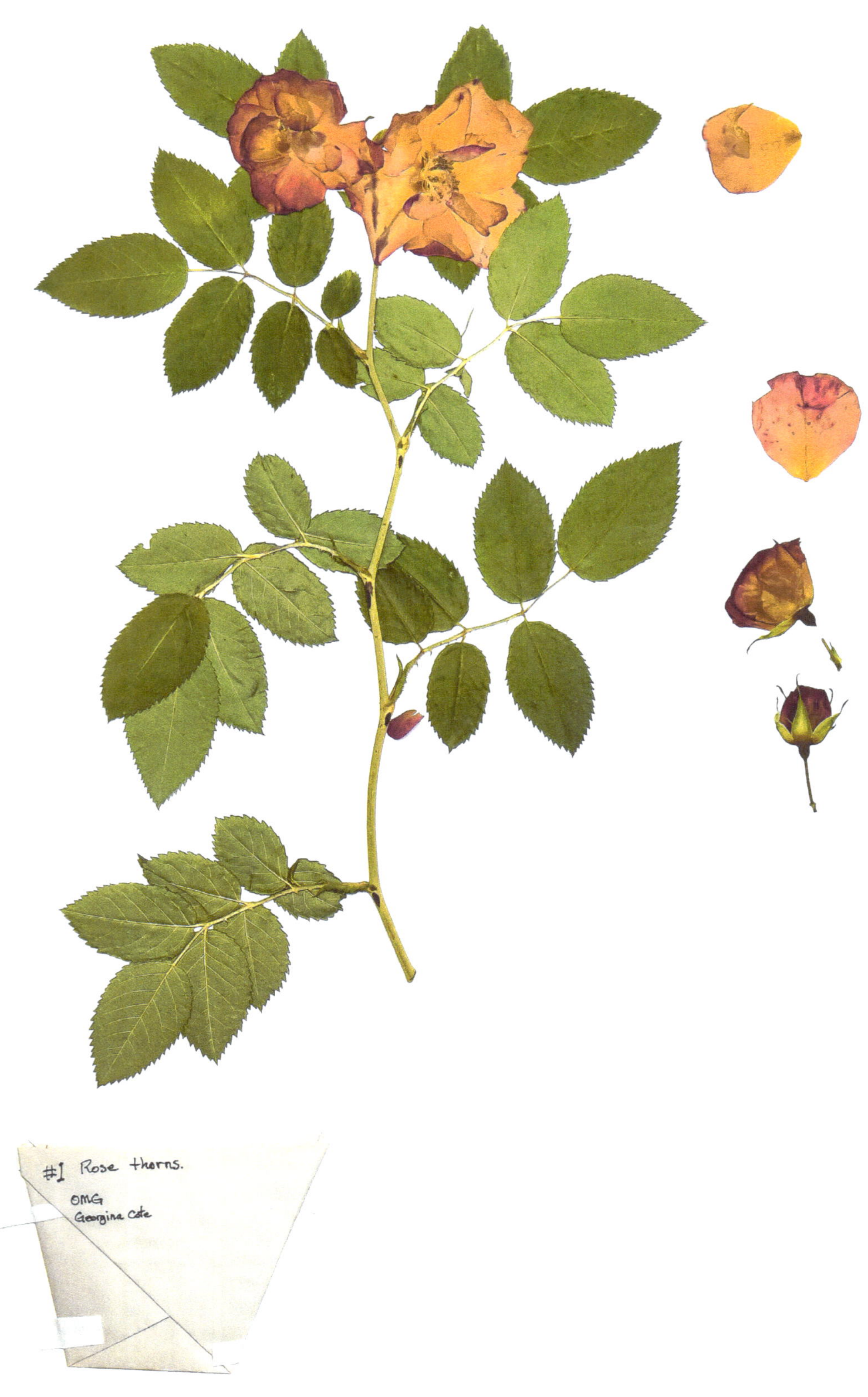

#1 Rose thorns.
OMG
Georgina Cate

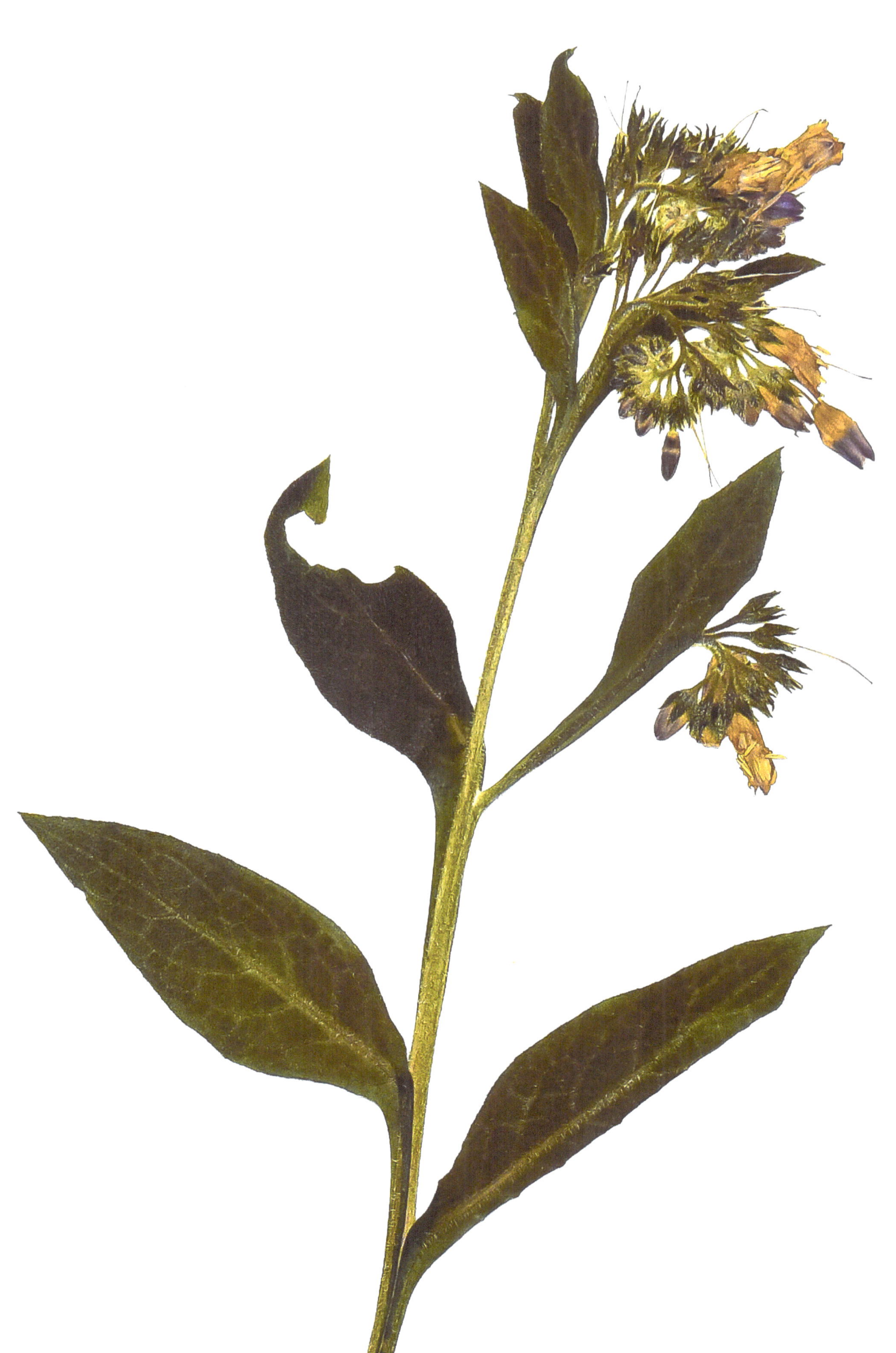

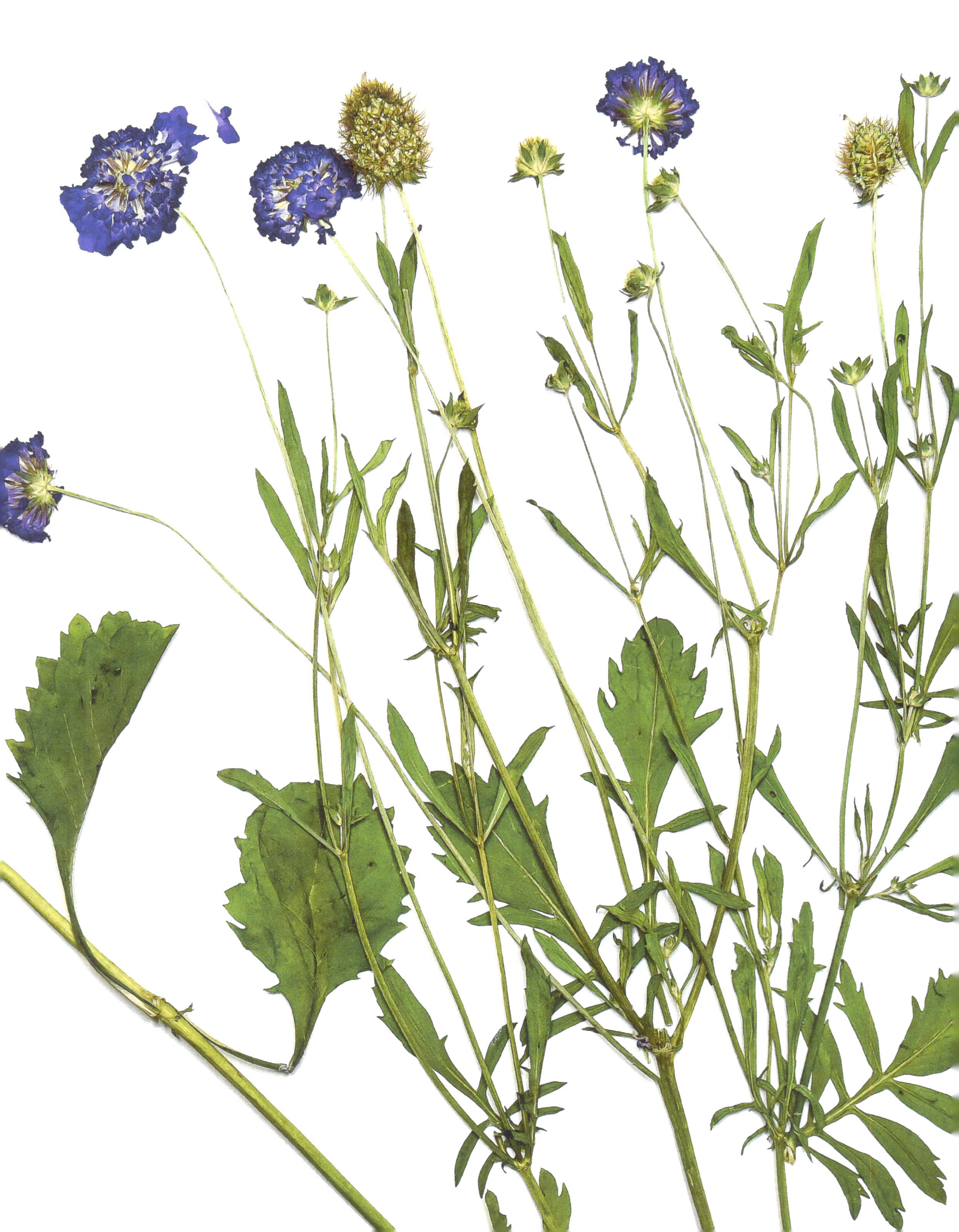

"Human health is inseparable from soil health."
– William Albrecht

Chair of the Department of Soils, University of Missouri

When we understand the complexities of nature and see that all of nature is covered and filled with biodiversity, we realize that what applies to the plants also applies to the animals, and to us. Any attack on nature is an attack on us.

shinrin-yoku n. Japanese tradition of "forest bathing" or silent wandering through a forest as a break from the distractions and stresses of our world.

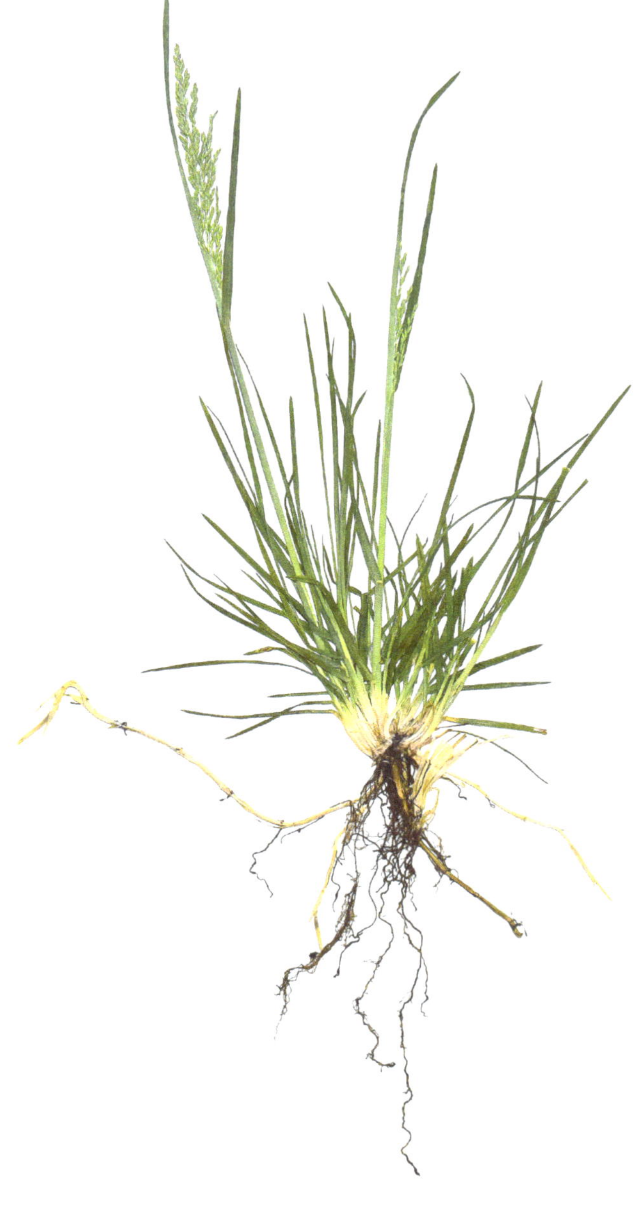

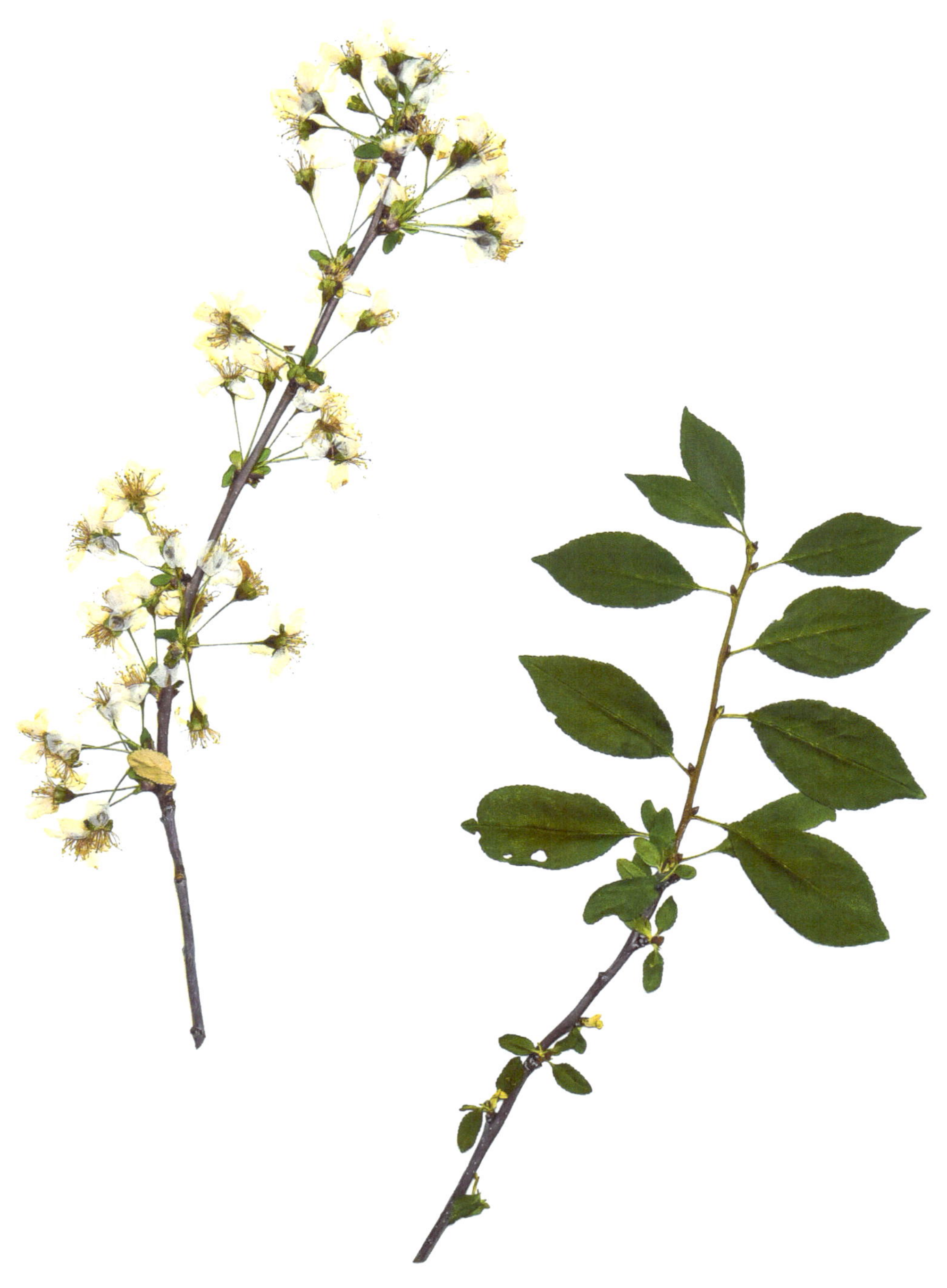

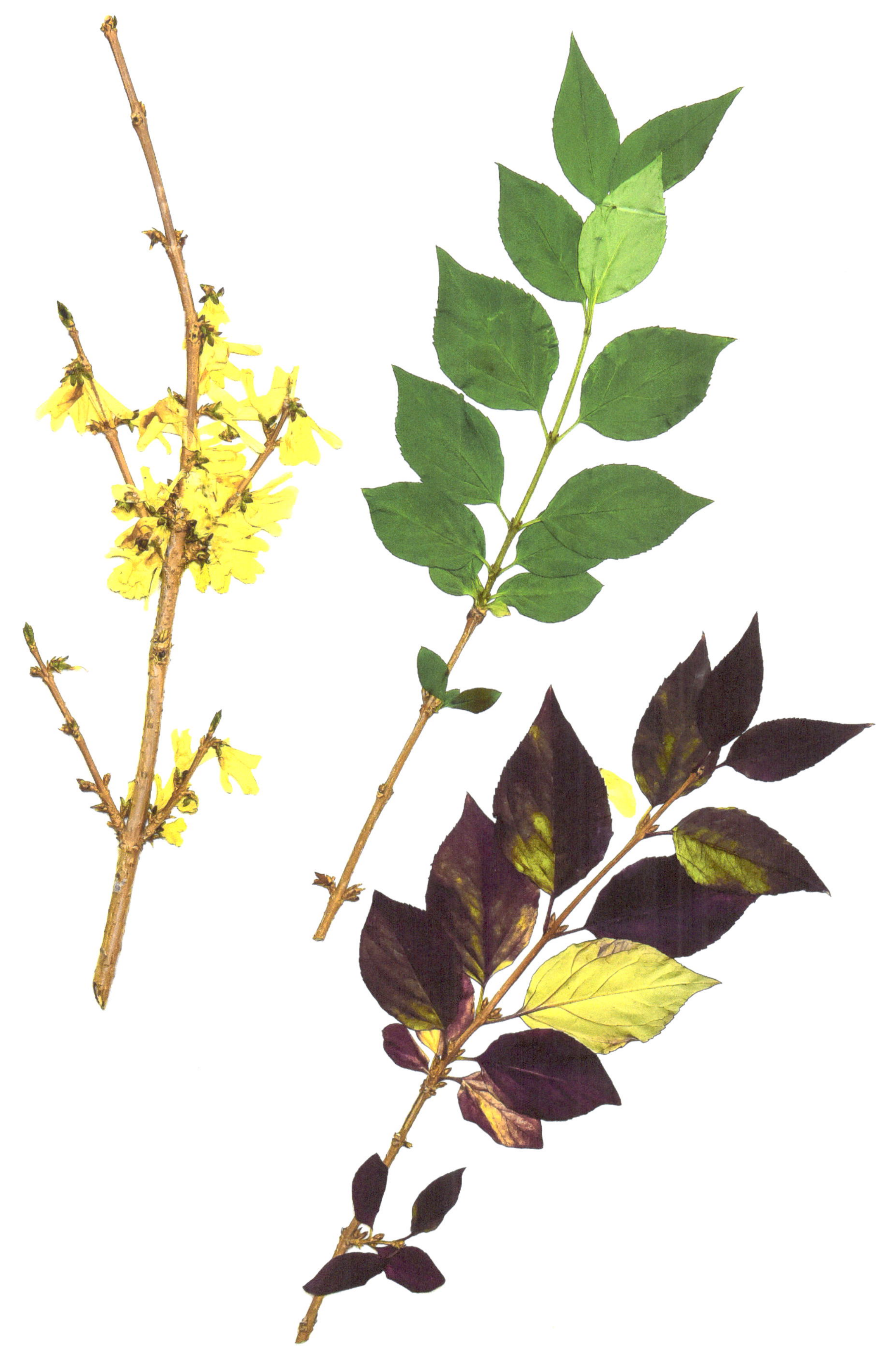

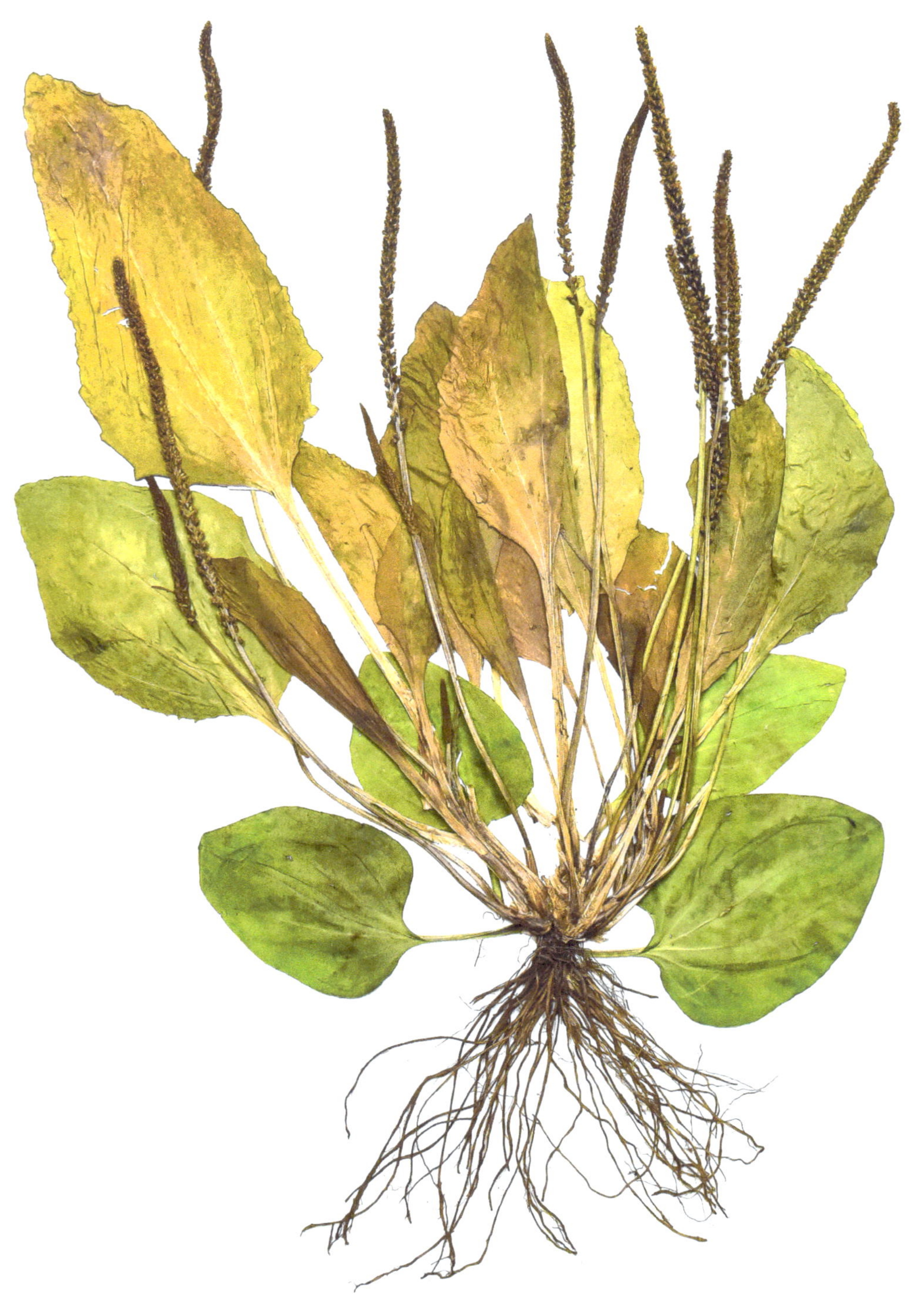

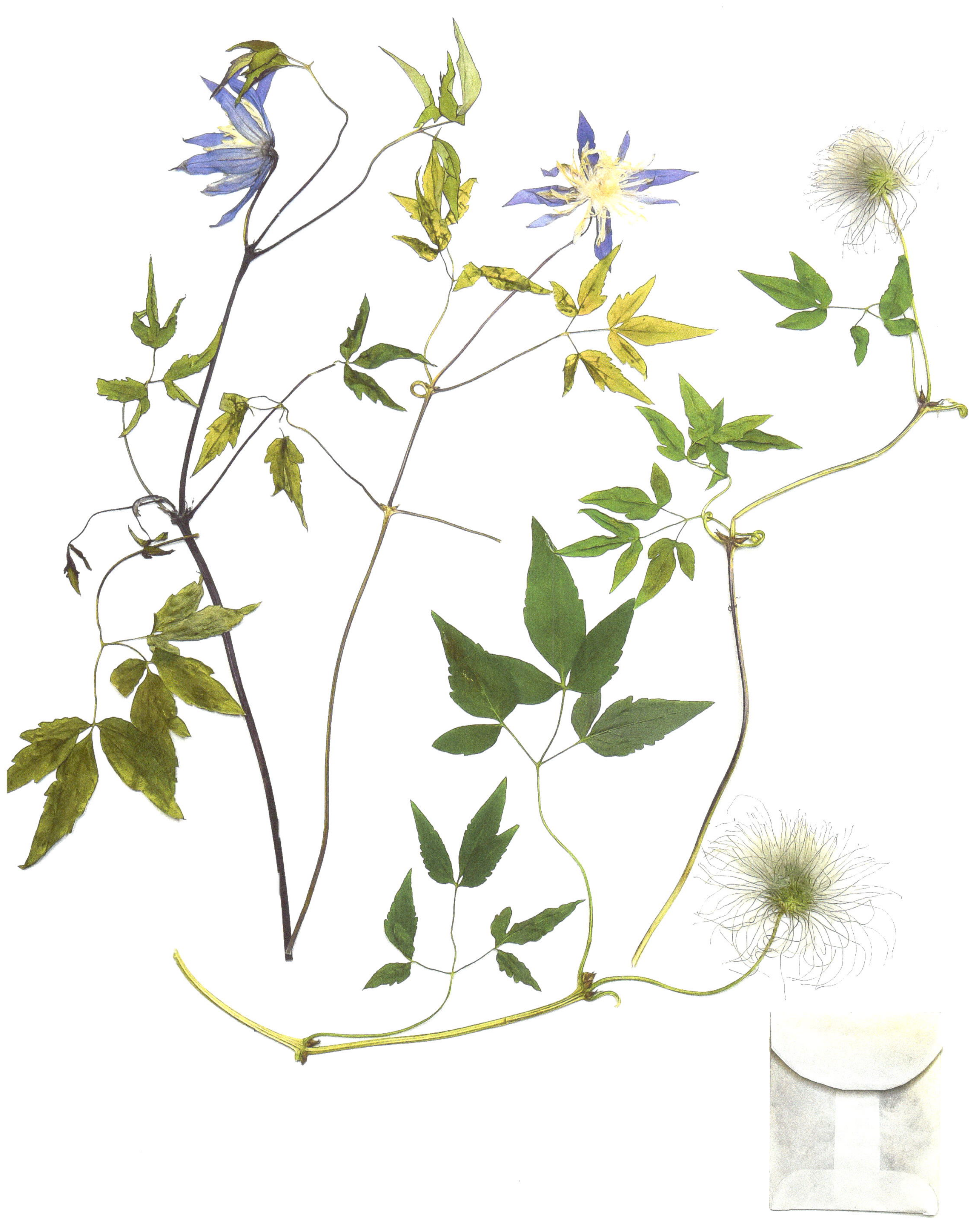

Ten Largest Herbaria

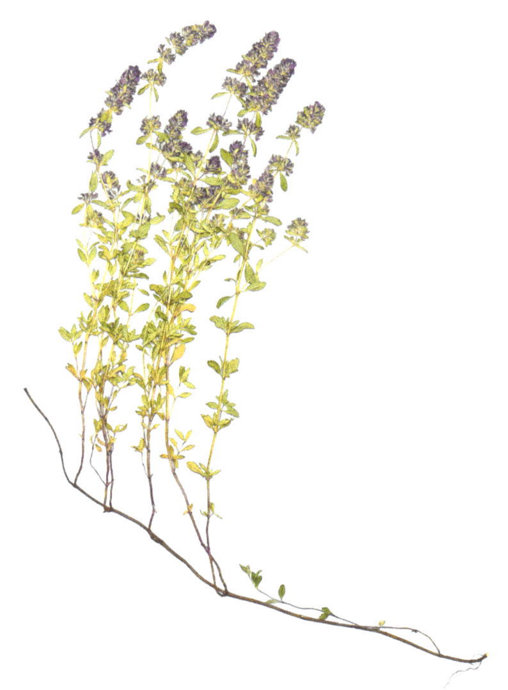

At present, the most extensive collections are located at:

- Museum National d'Histoire Naturelle (Paris, France)
- New York Botanical Garden (Bronx, New York, USA)
- Komarov Botanical Institute (St. Petersburg, Russia)
- Royal Botanic Gardens (Kew, England, UK)
- Conservatoire et Jardin Botaniques de la Ville de Geneve (Geneva, Switzerland)
- Missouri Botanical Garden (St. Louis, Missouri, USA)
- British Museum of Natural History (London, England, UK)
- Harvard University (Cambridge, Massachusetts, USA)
- Swedish Museum of Natural History (Stockholm, Sweden)
- United States National Herbarium (Washington, DC, USA)

Our Provincial Herbarium is located at the Royal Alberta Museum in Edmonton, and our National Herbarium is located at the Canadian Museum of Nature in Ottawa.

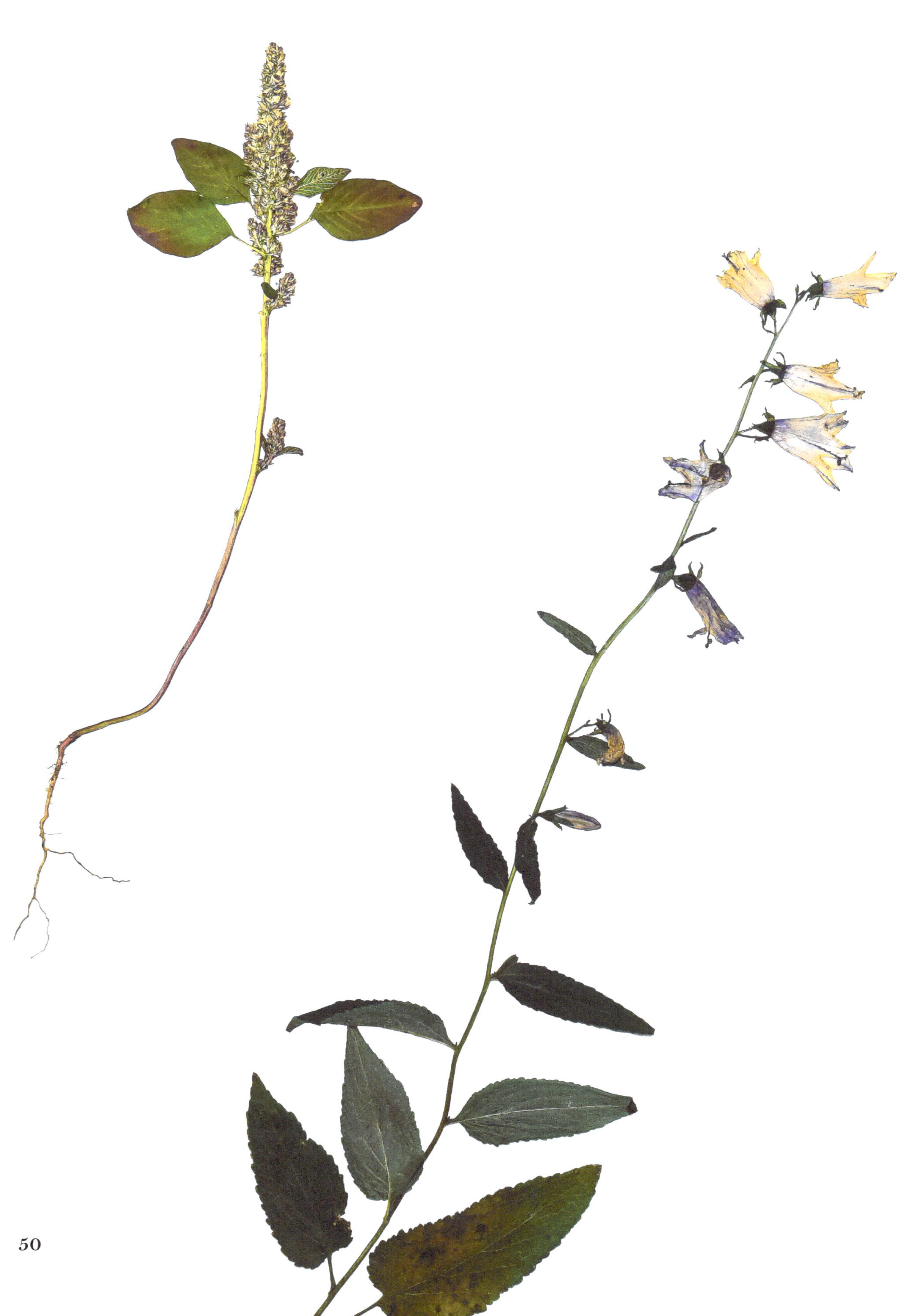

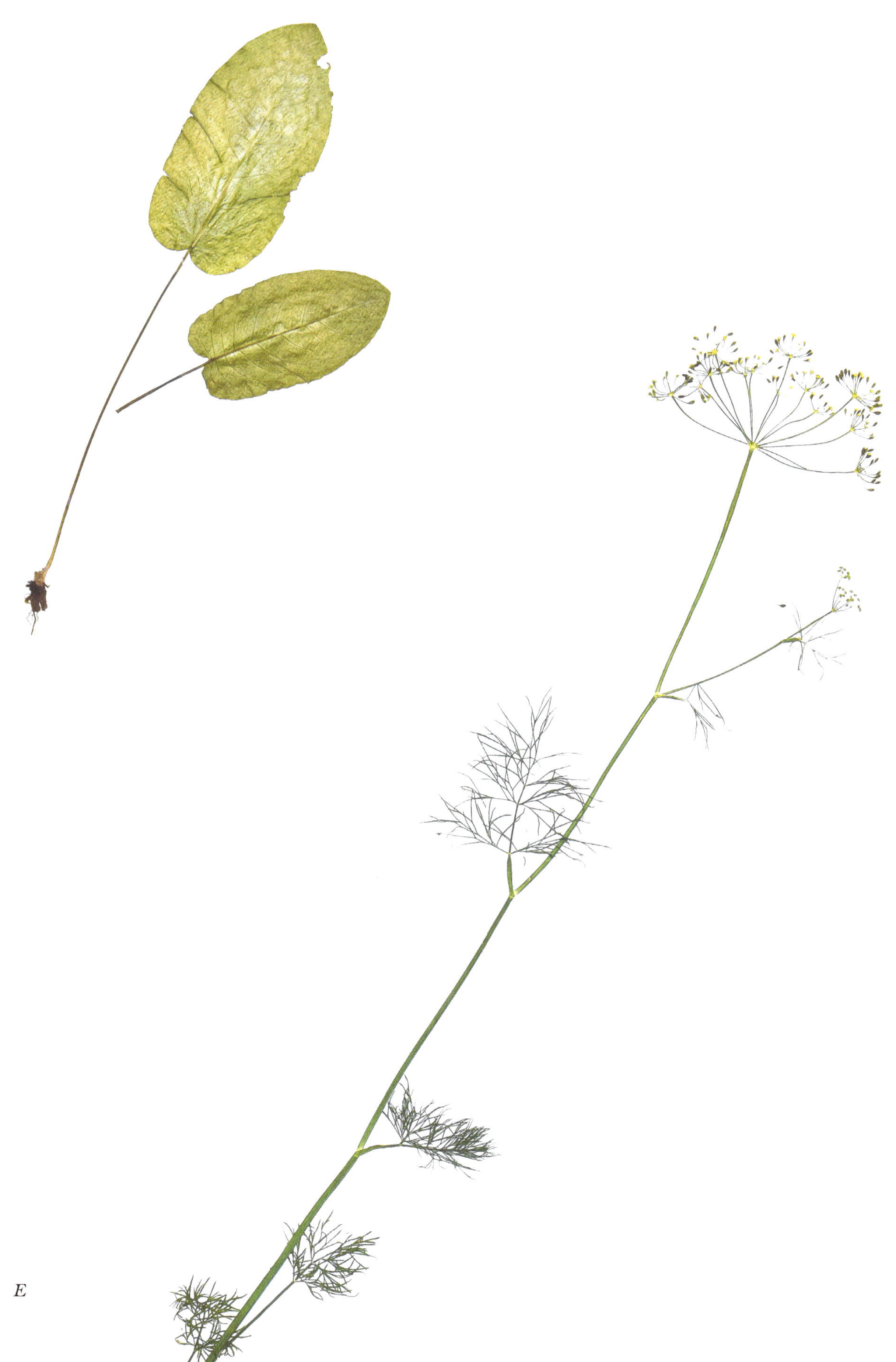

E

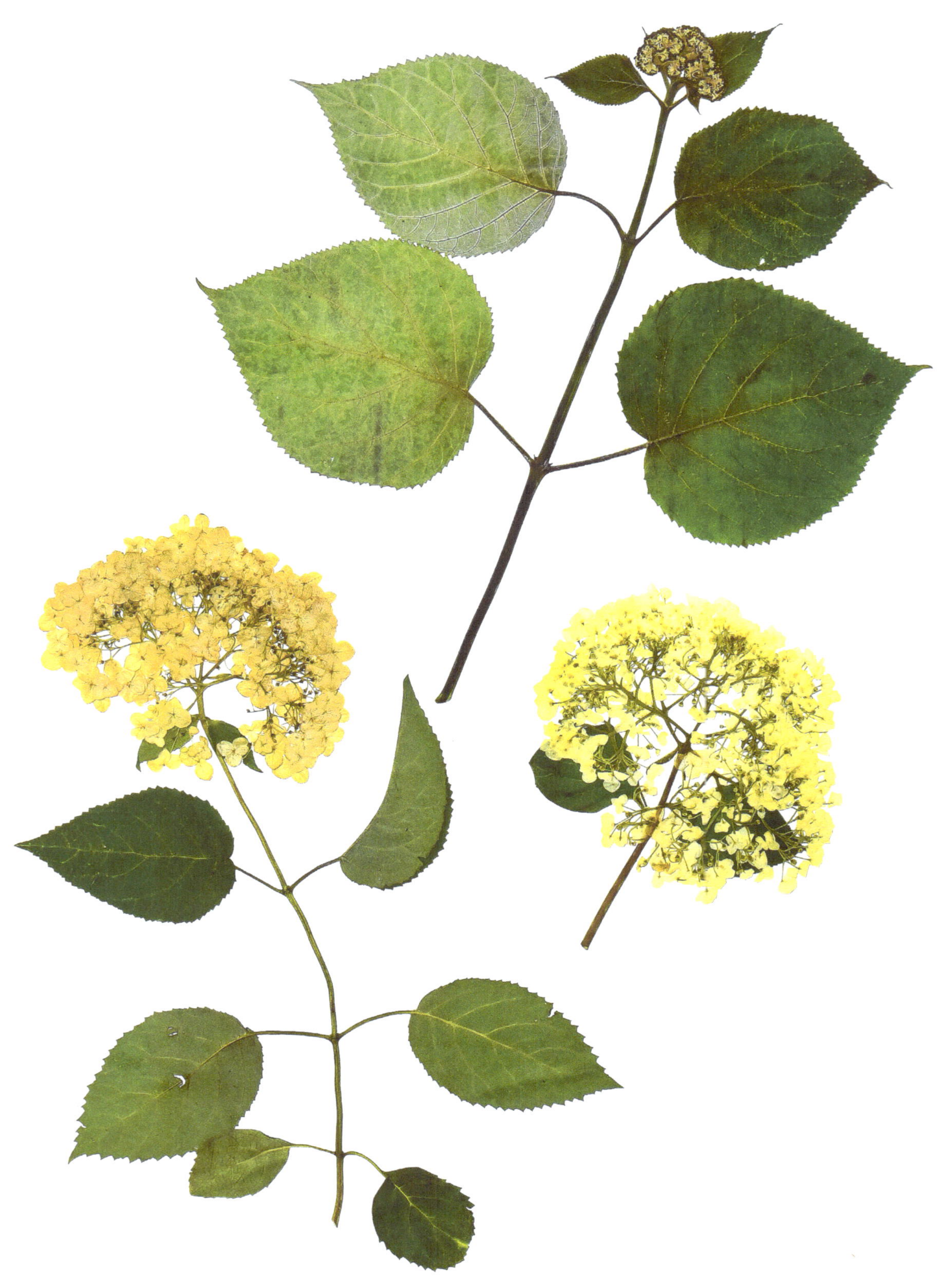

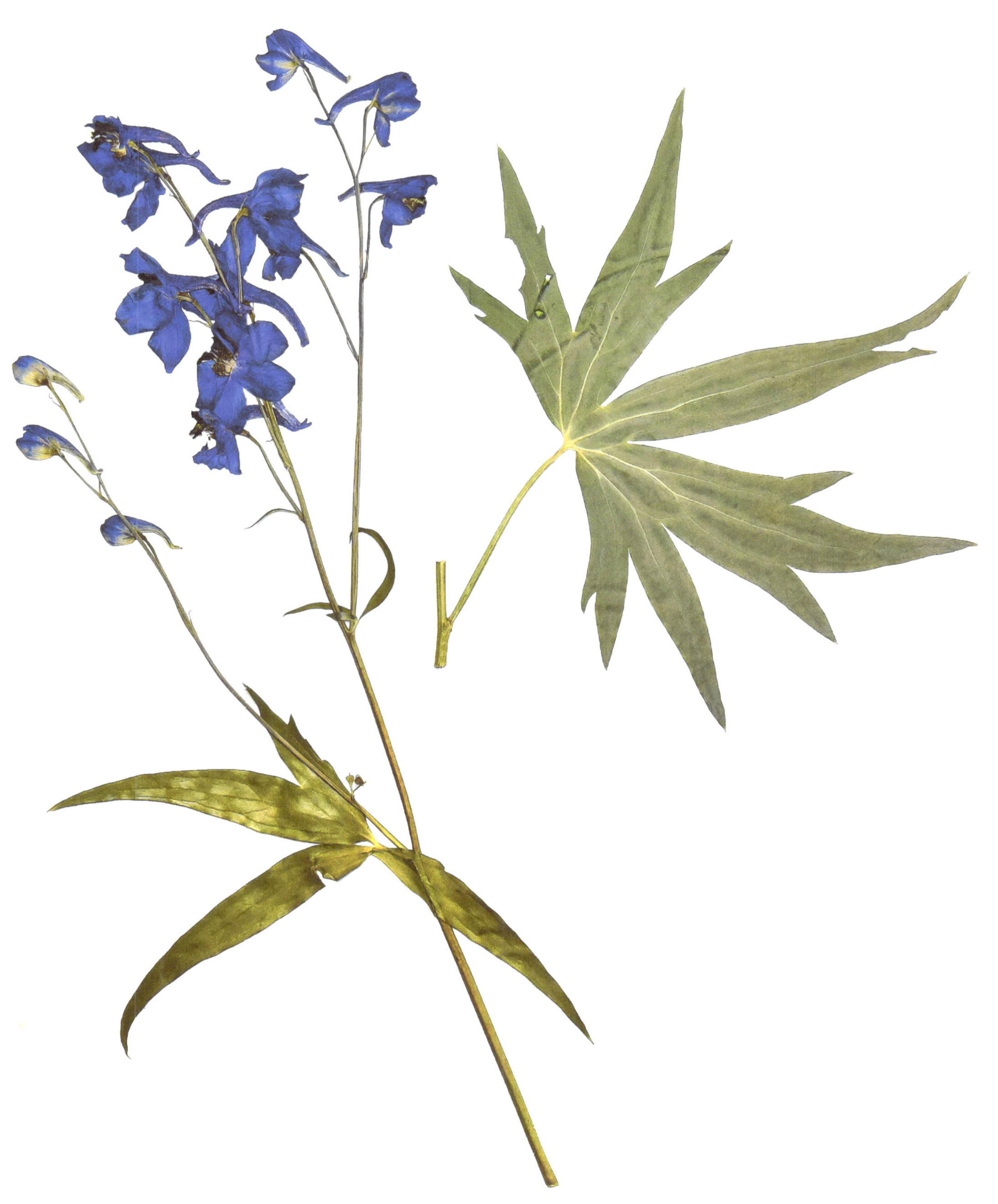

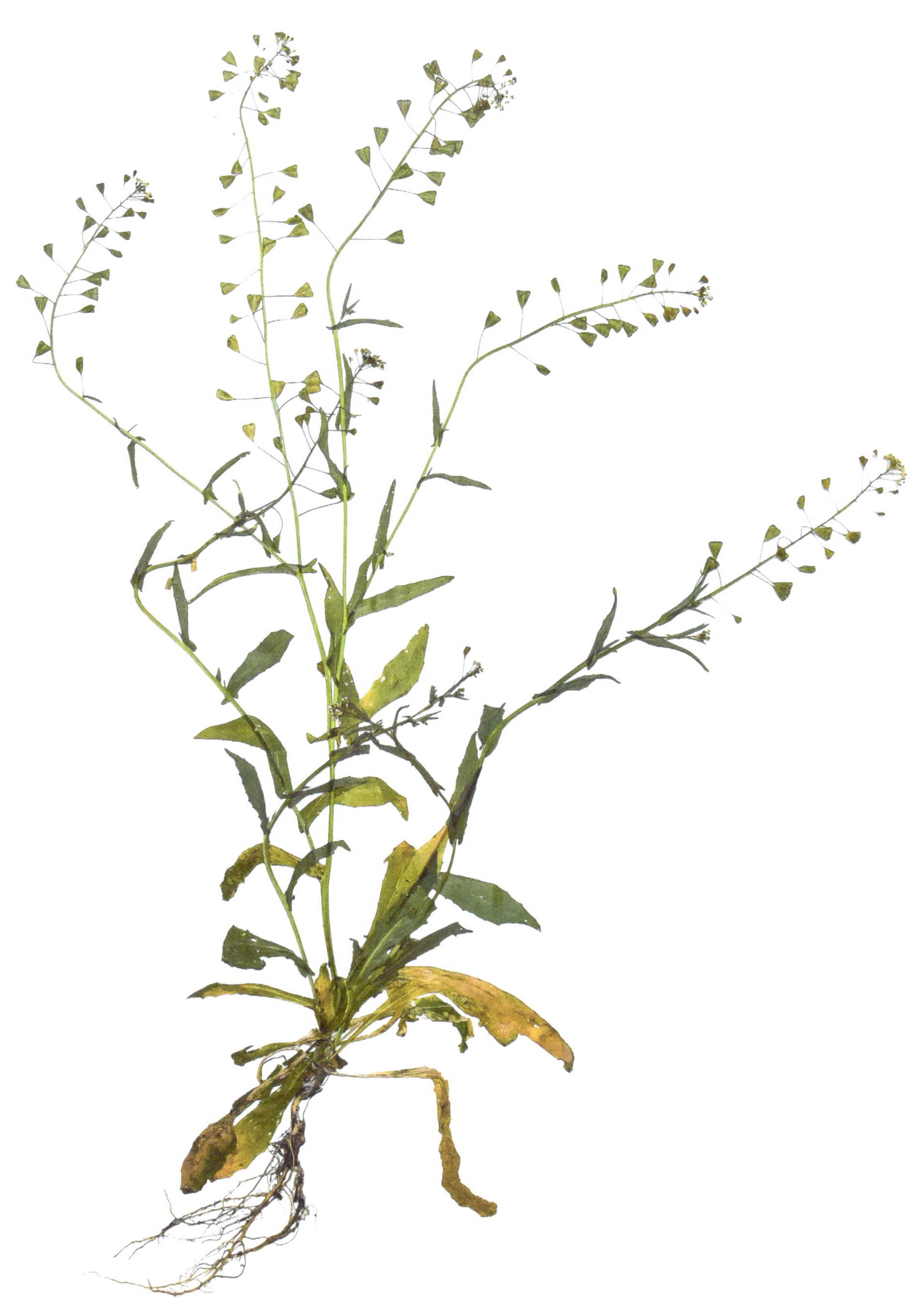

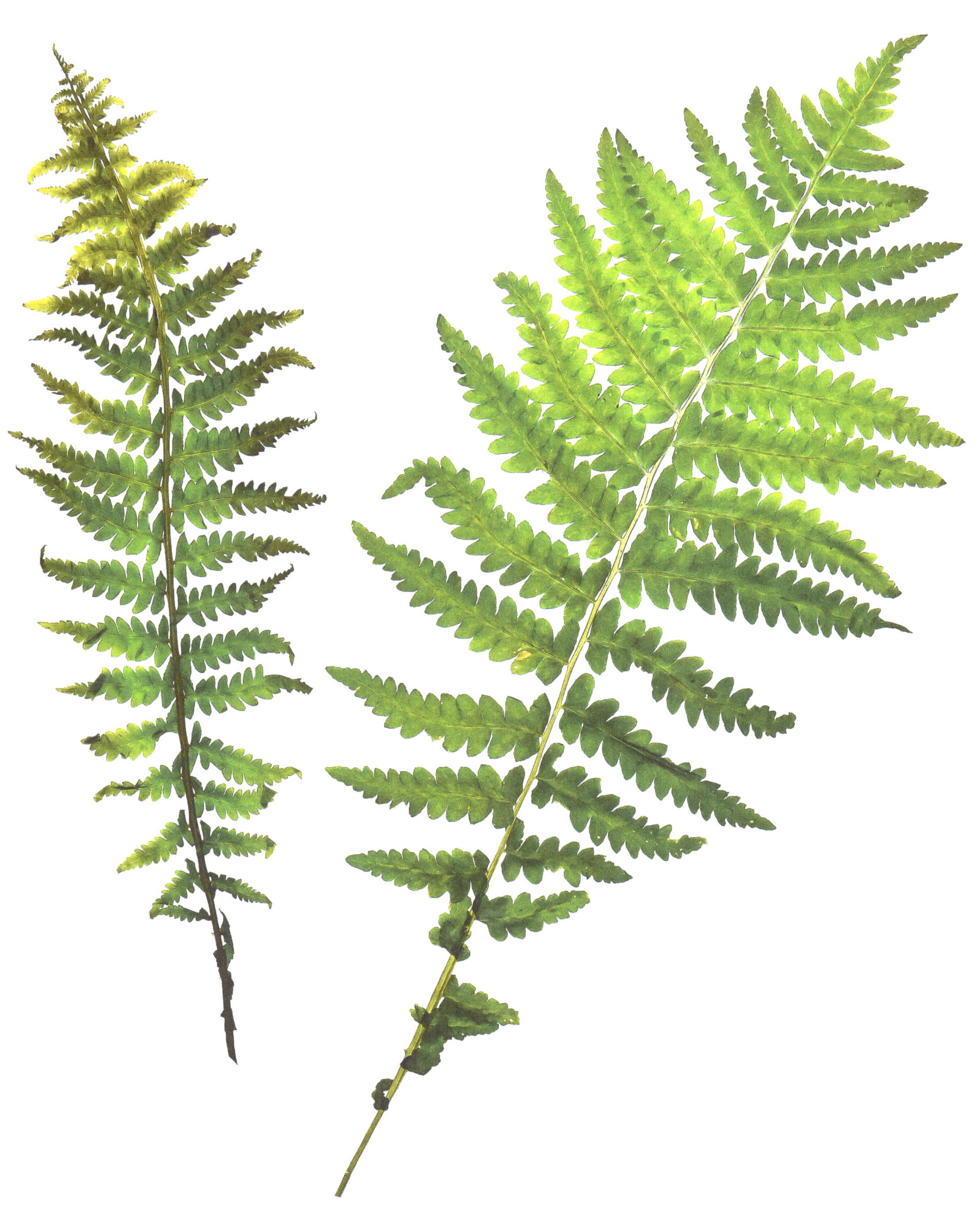

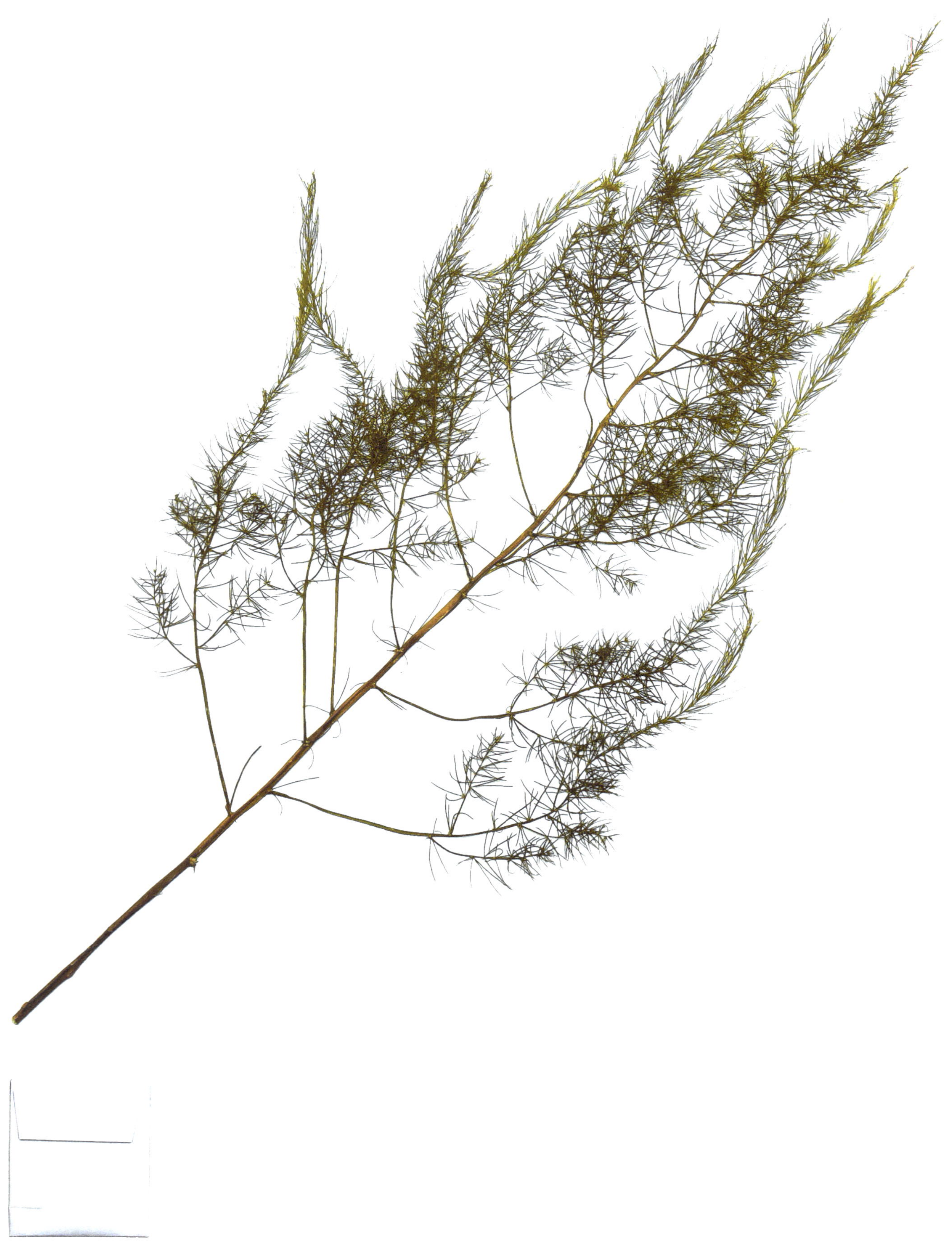

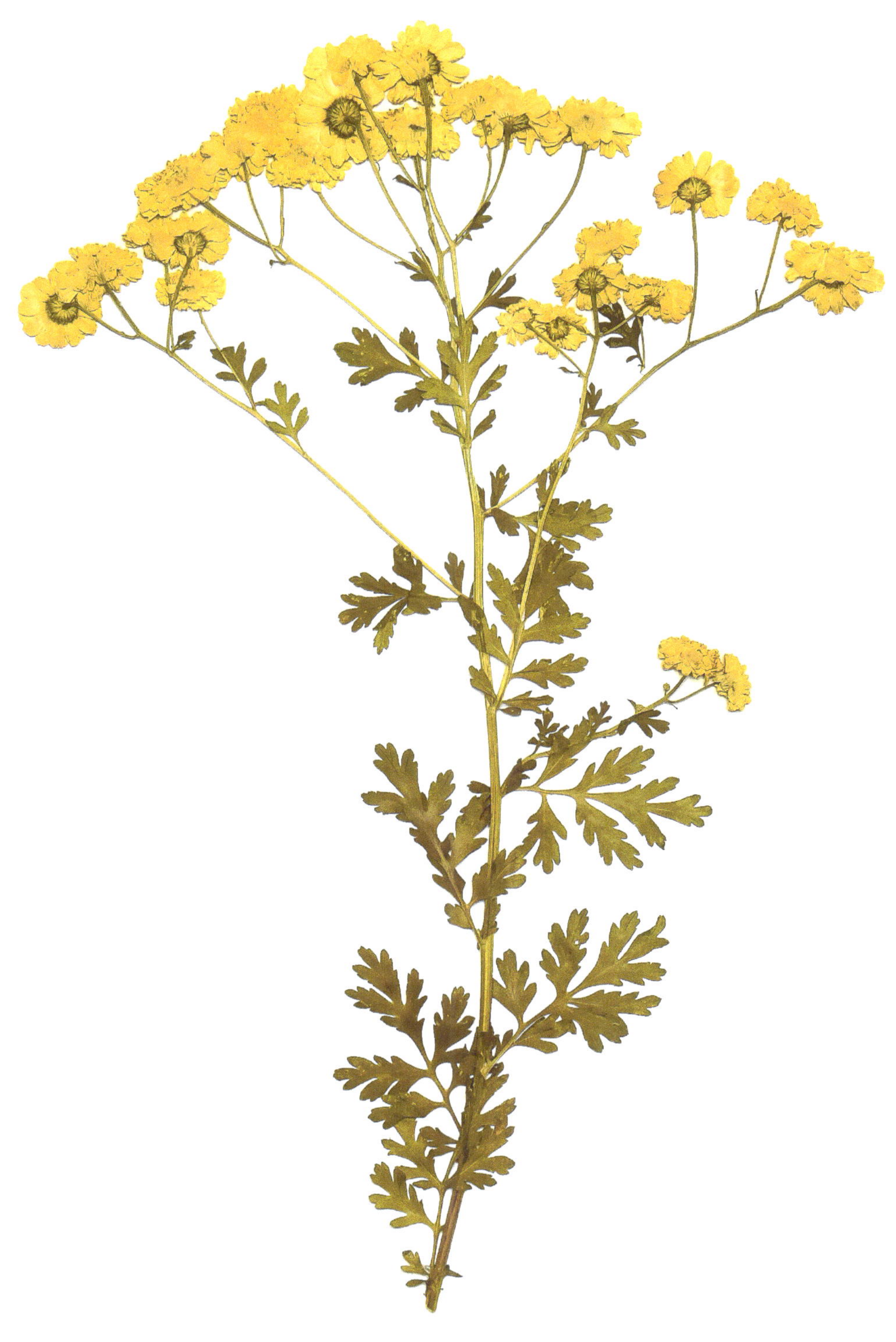

"What's in a name? that which we call a rose / By any other name would smell as sweet"

– William Shakespeare, *Romeo and Juliet*

Carl Linnaeus, one of the most famous botanists in history, developed the system of binomial nomenclature: the scientific naming of all living things. Without Linnaeus, plants, animals, and fungi might have very different names, although Juliet would not have let that stop her. Plants are grouped into families based on common characteristics. The Asters have multiple flowers surrounded by rays, like a Sunflower or Daisy. The Rose family not only has edible fruit but also has a way of defending itself against herbivores. Contrary to popular belief, there is no plant family called "weeds."

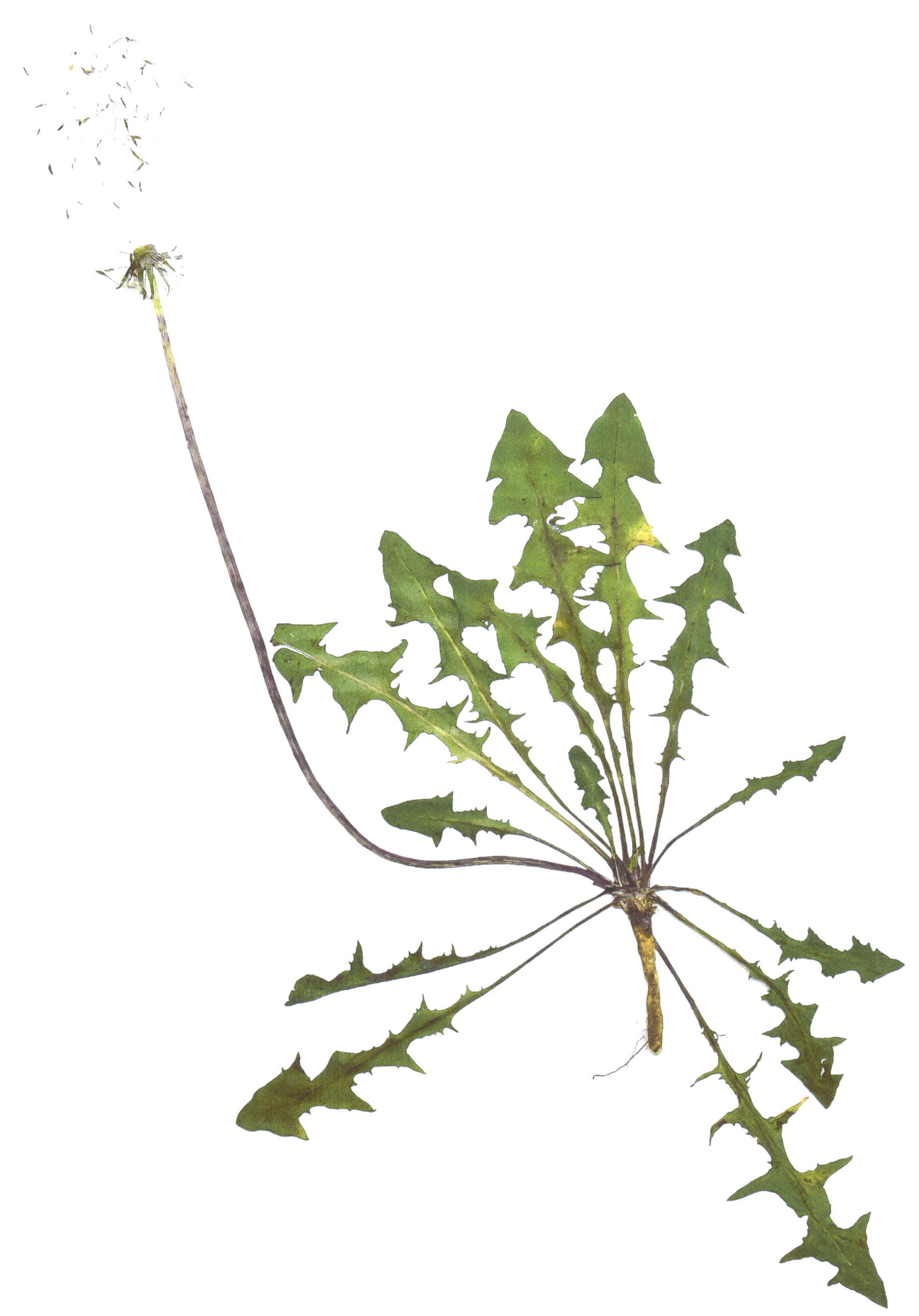

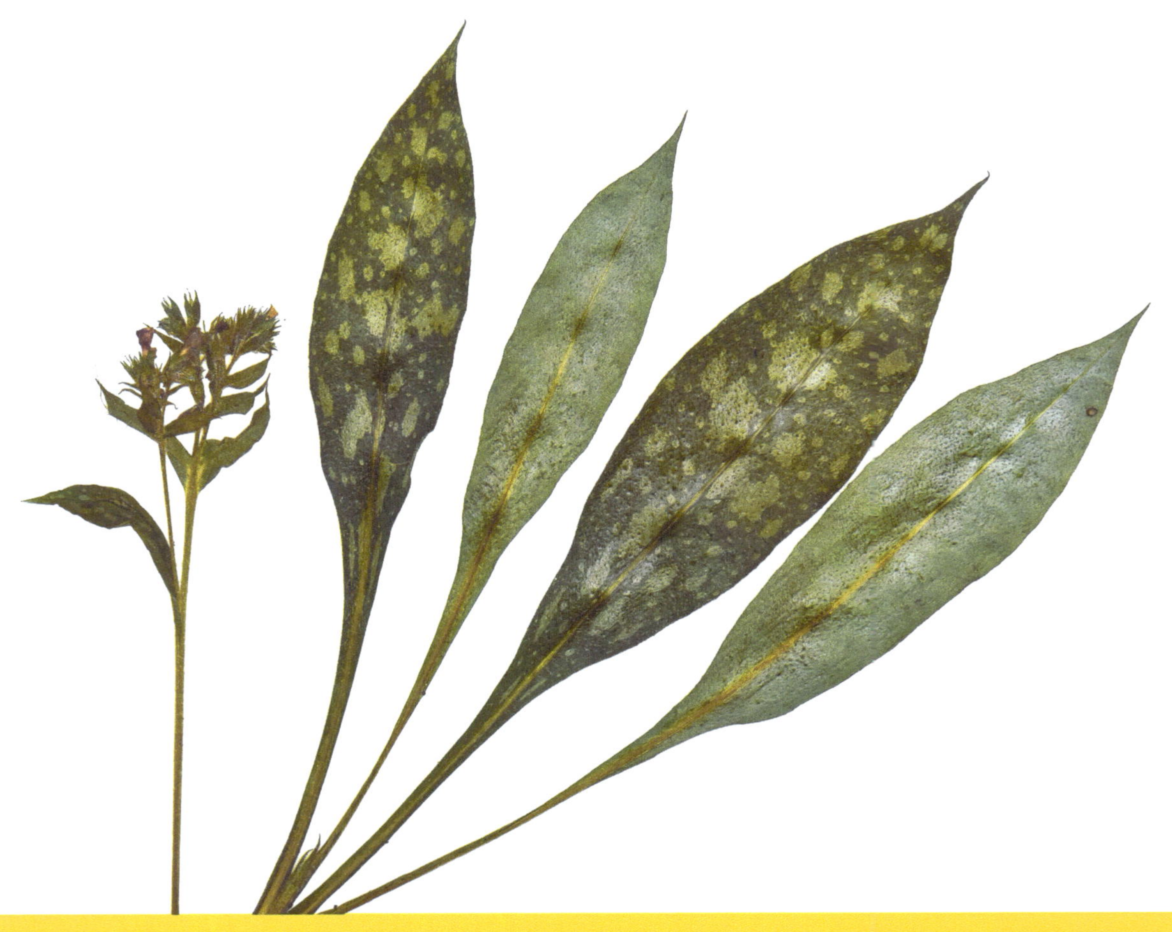

"Nature has always been fertilizing with the organic matter which is dropped back to the soil from the previous plant generations. Organic matter is still the most reliable fertilizer in terms of the nutrient ratios and of the time when maximums must be delivered."

- John Kempf, 2020

https://johnkempf.com/organic-matter-the-constitution-of-the-soil/

Not only are plant residues beautiful and educational, but also valuable to soil.

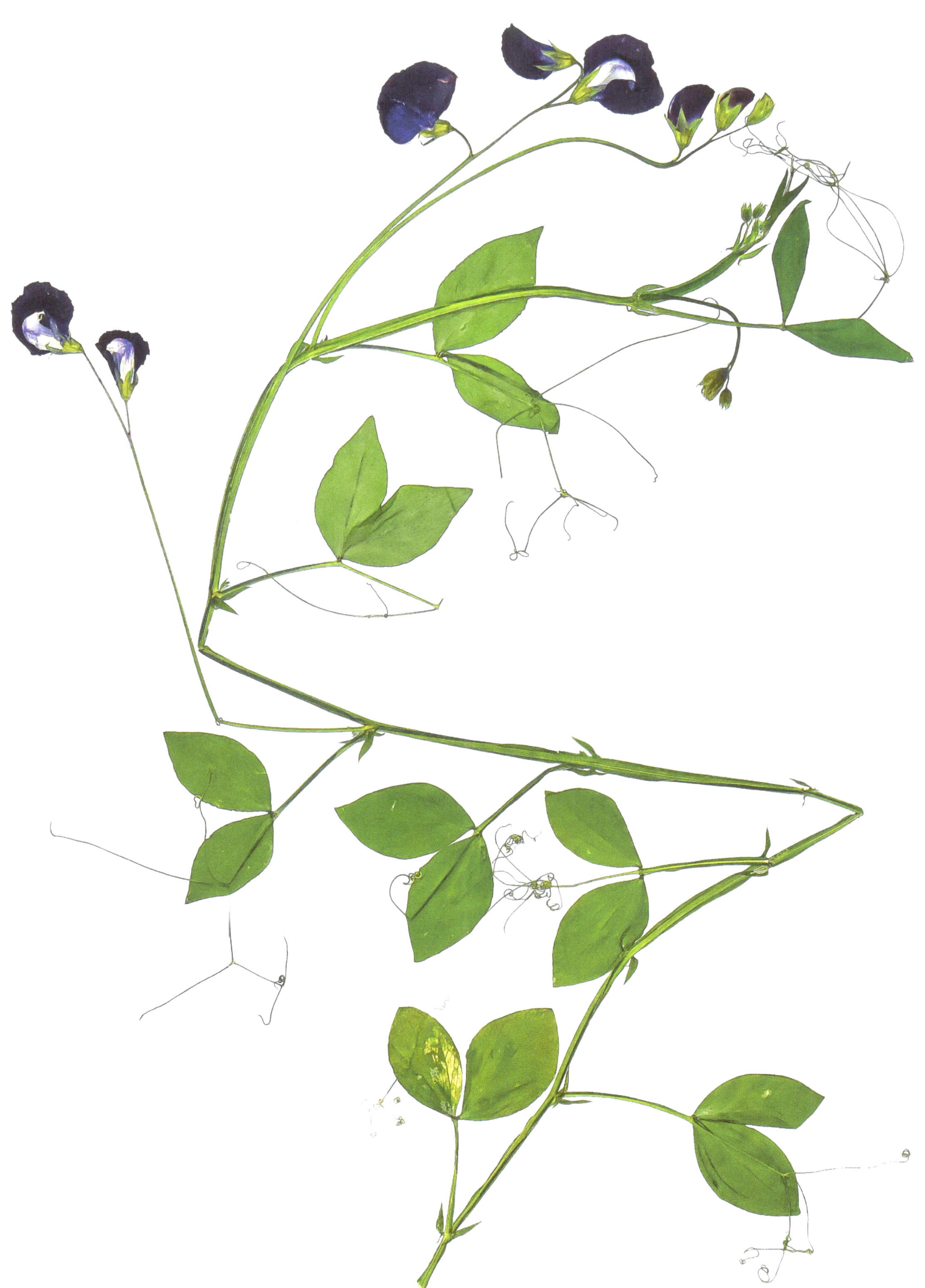

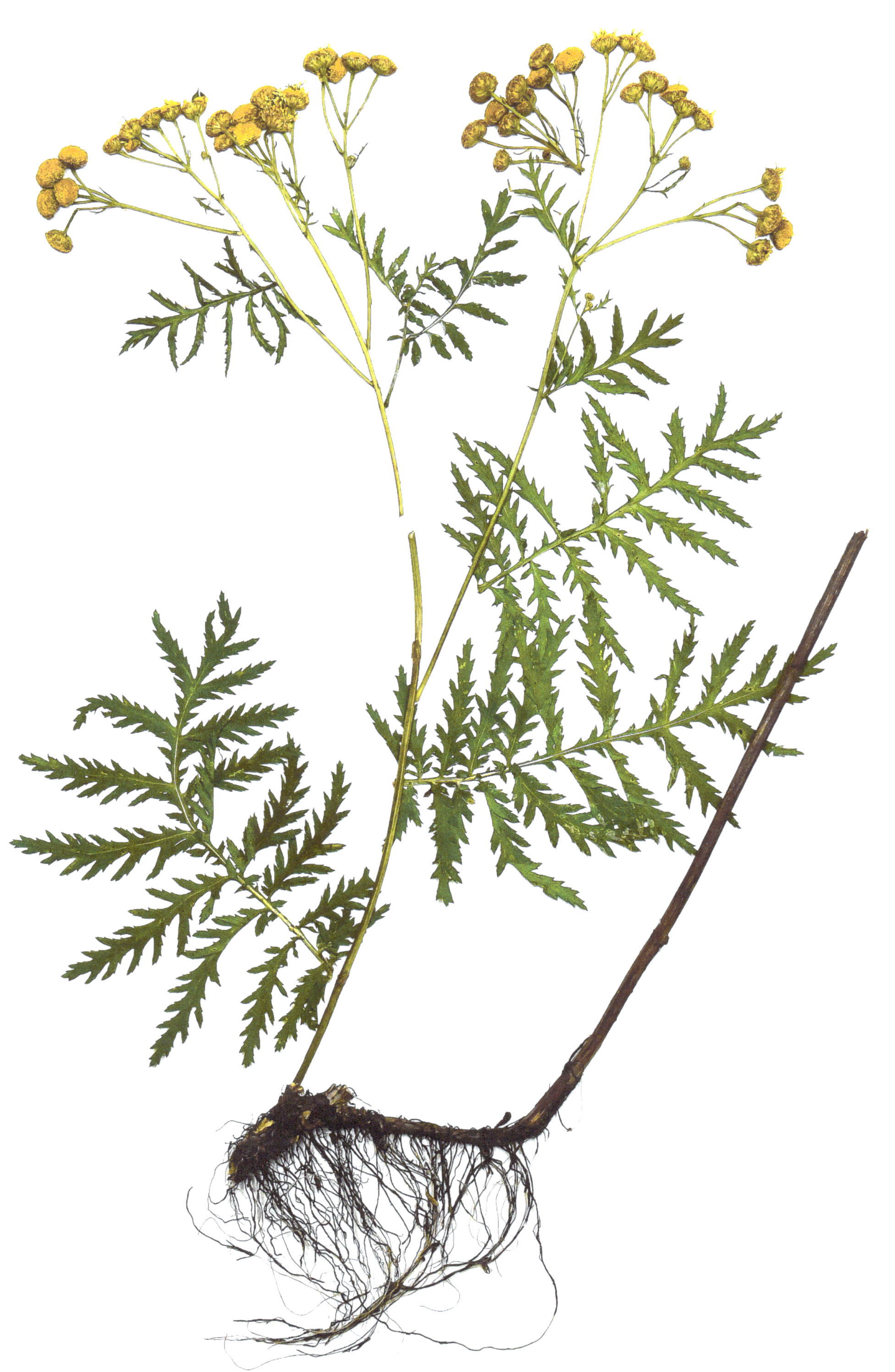

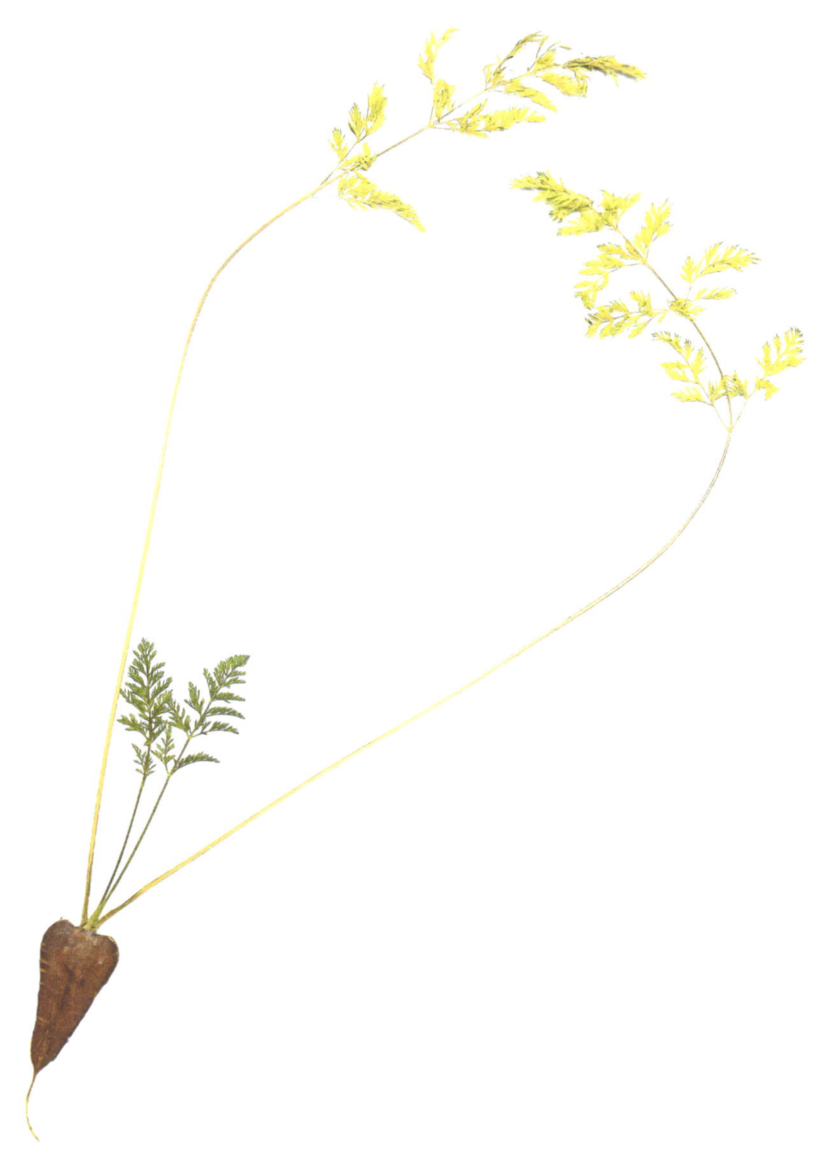

As gardeners move towards a more natural approach to gardening, we are realizing that fall clean-up—power raking, aerating, tilling, and fertilizing—does more damage than nature can cope with. Next time autumn rolls around, perhaps think to yourself, "Less is more."

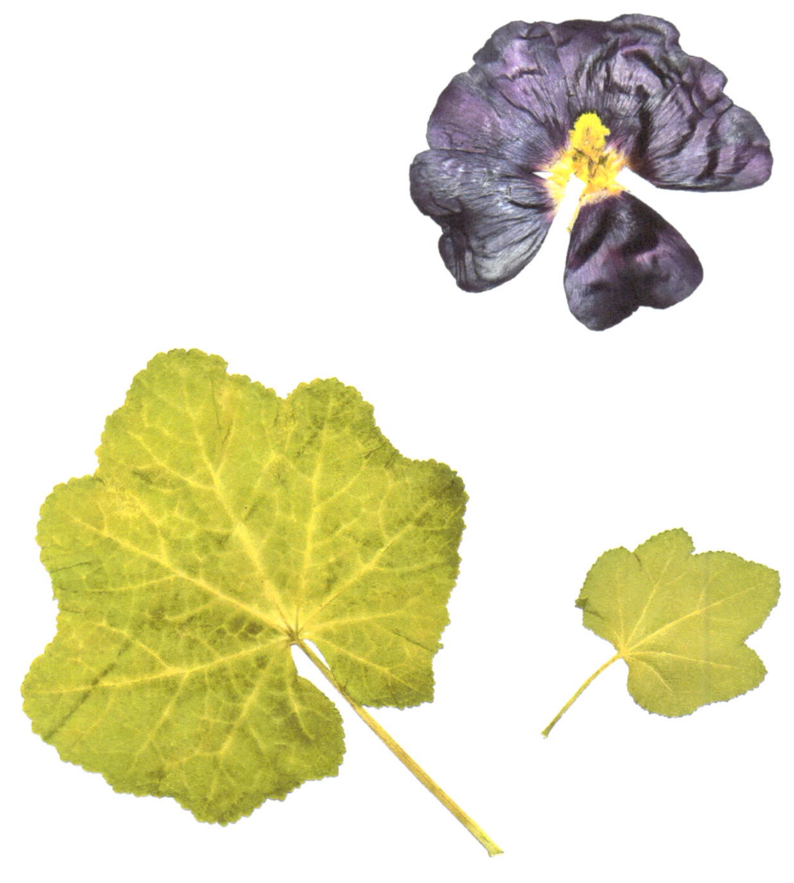

We have been taught to treat plant residues as litter—waste materials to be discarded. Heidi Hermary notes that nature's wonder "comes to a halt when we deprive the soil dwelling organisms of their primary carbohydrate source: the old and discarded plant parts," but the real joy of a thick blanket of residues is the spring emergence of butter-flies, bees, ladybugs, and lacewings.

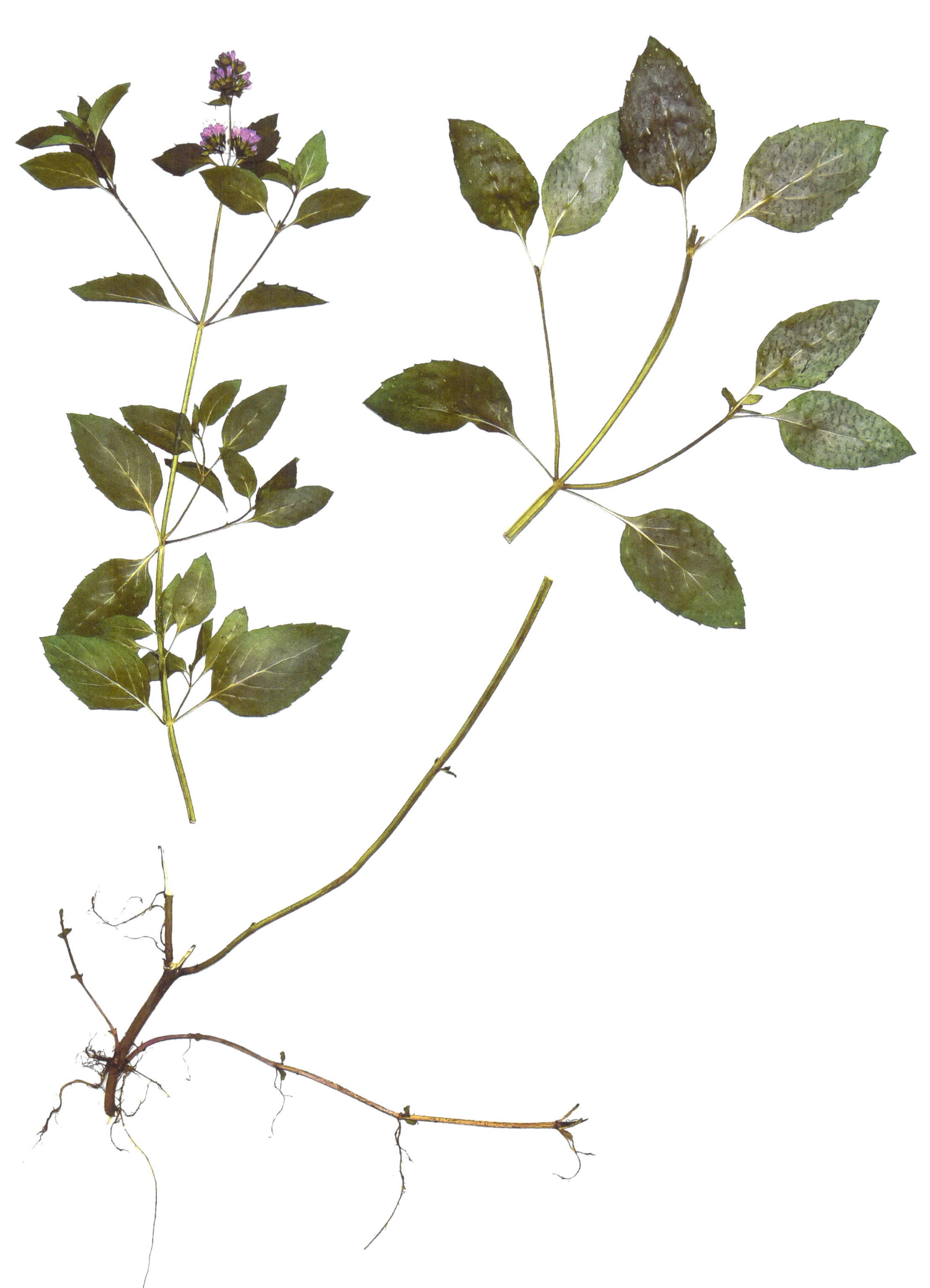

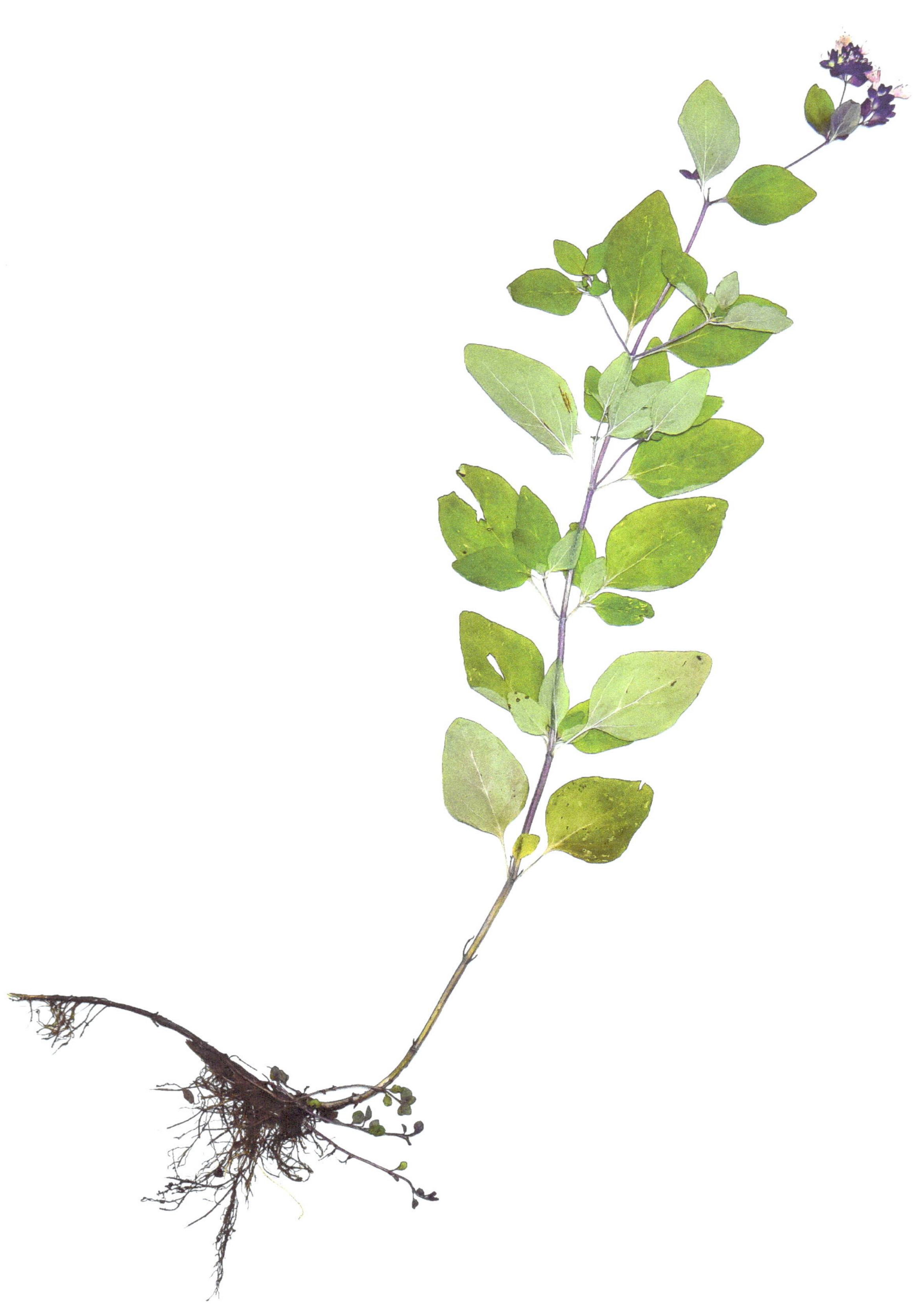

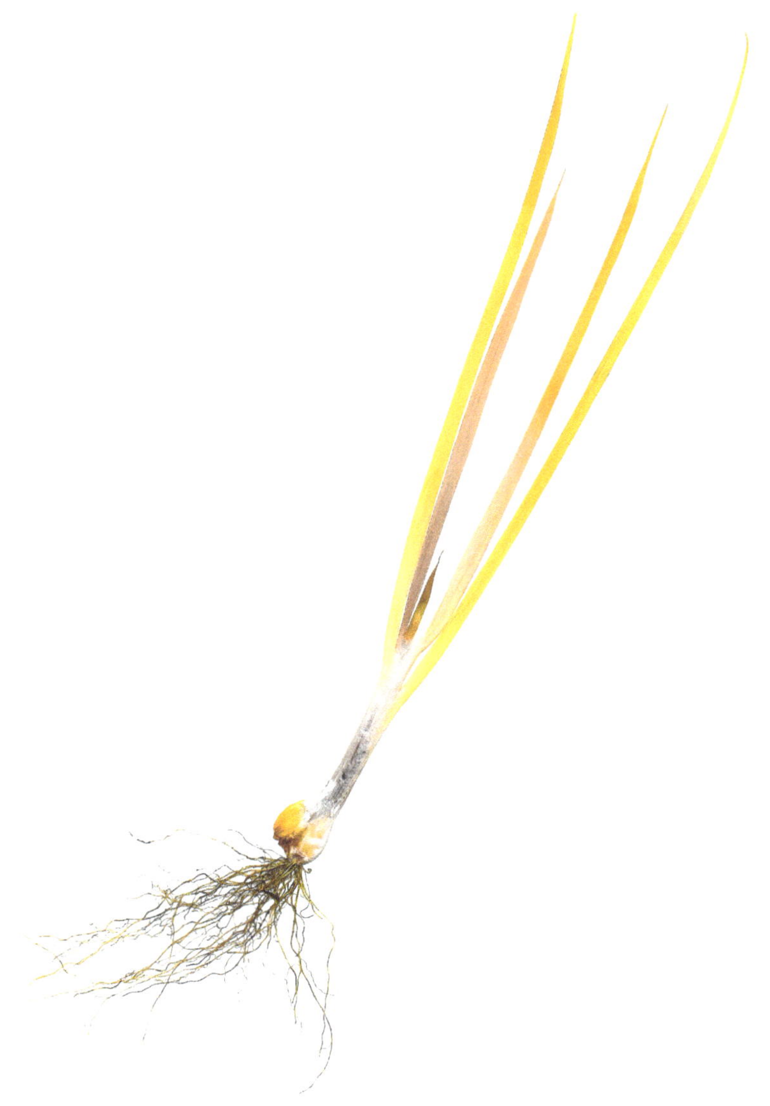

Beautiful flowers and healthy plants are the outcome of many complex and inter-related sciences. Rather than learning the details of OM, CEC, pH, Eh, PSMs, and memorizing the periodic table, the OMG students are given straightforward and actionable guidelines. Their greatest challenge is to forget what they already know.

Harvesting

*"We can complain because rose bushes have thorns,
or rejoice because thorn bushes have roses."*

- Abraham Lincoln

There is no wrong time to press plants, but capturing vivid colours in the bloom depends on collecting specimens when the bloom is freshly opened, pressing them tightly, and then drying the plants quickly. Let your specimen be an expression of your feelings in that moment. Your specimen will press better and last longer if the plant is not stressed.

For more scientifically valuable specimens:

- Photograph the plant and the surrounding area.
- Pause to ask if the plant should be taken.
  If only a few are present, take only the photo.
- Take a typical specimen. Get all parts of the plant, including some of the root.
- Place the specimen and all collected parts into a plastic bag.
  Include a reference tag that corresponds to your field notes.
- Take detailed field notes including:
  o Your name and the date
  o Location, latitude, longitude, and altitude
  o Surrounding vegetation
  o Plant Description and Notes
  o Habit and abundance
  o Any unusual observations
- Press the plant as quickly as possible.
- Inspect the plant every few days to monitor moisture. Dry thoroughly.
- Transfer your field notes to a label and glue it to the specimen when mounting your plant.

**What to Note on Your Label When
Collecting a Sample:**

- Plant Family
- Scientific Name
- Common Name
- Habitat
- Location
- Collector
- Date Collected

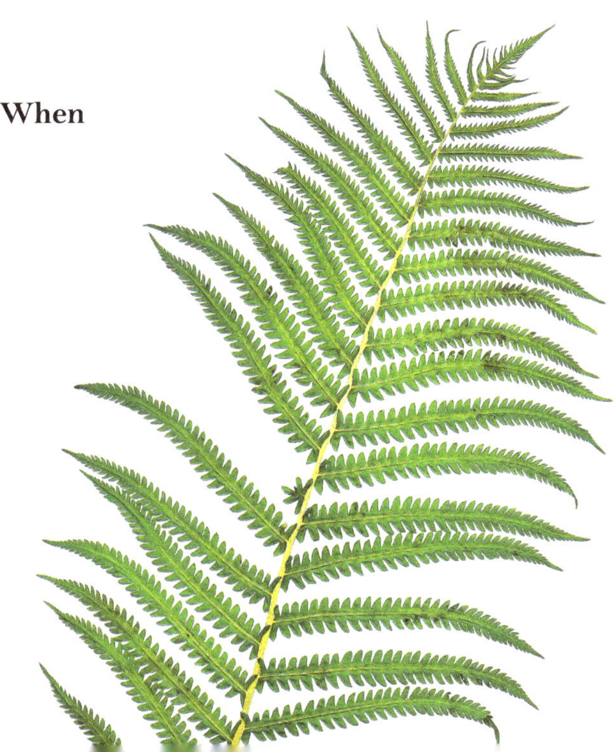

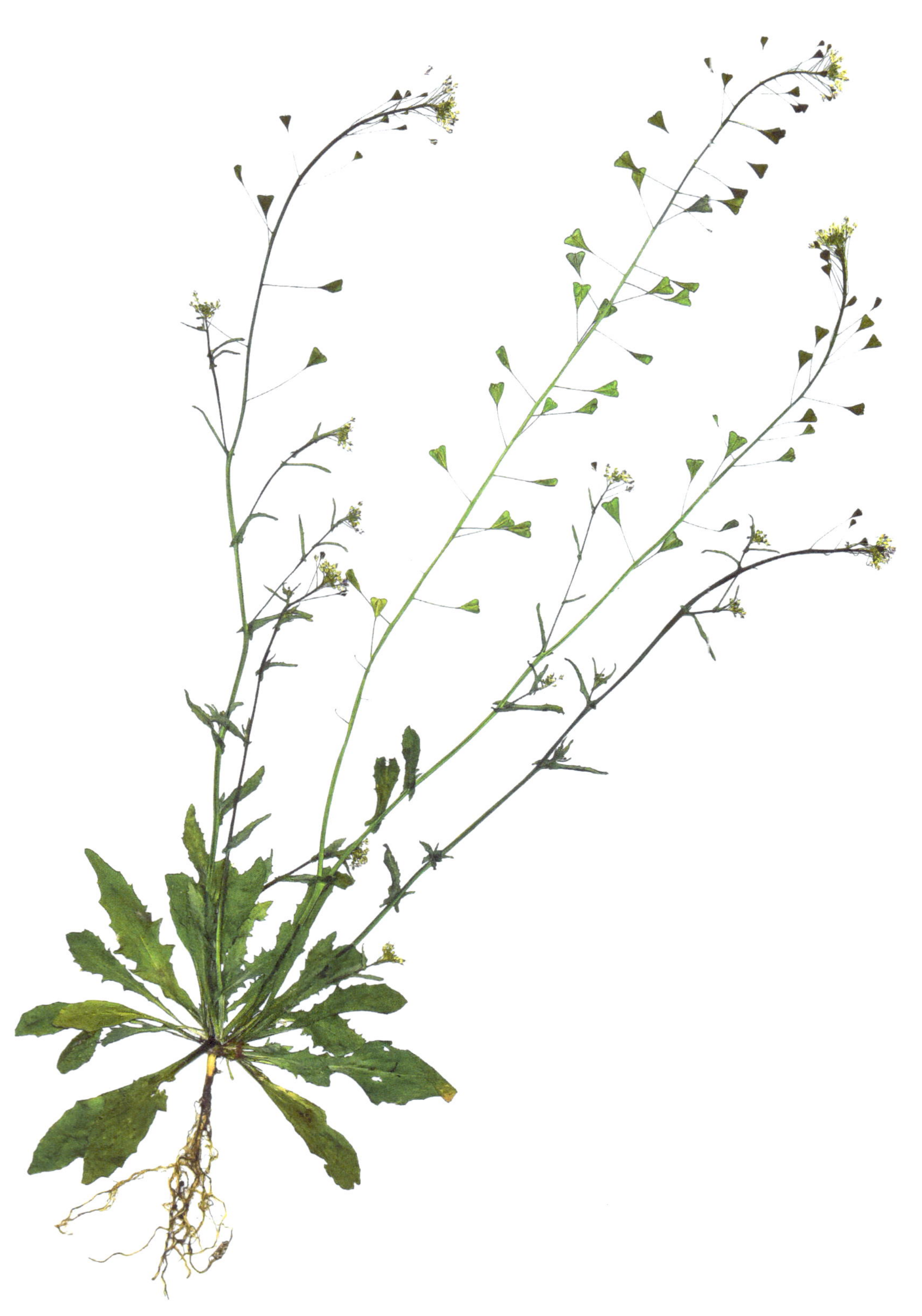

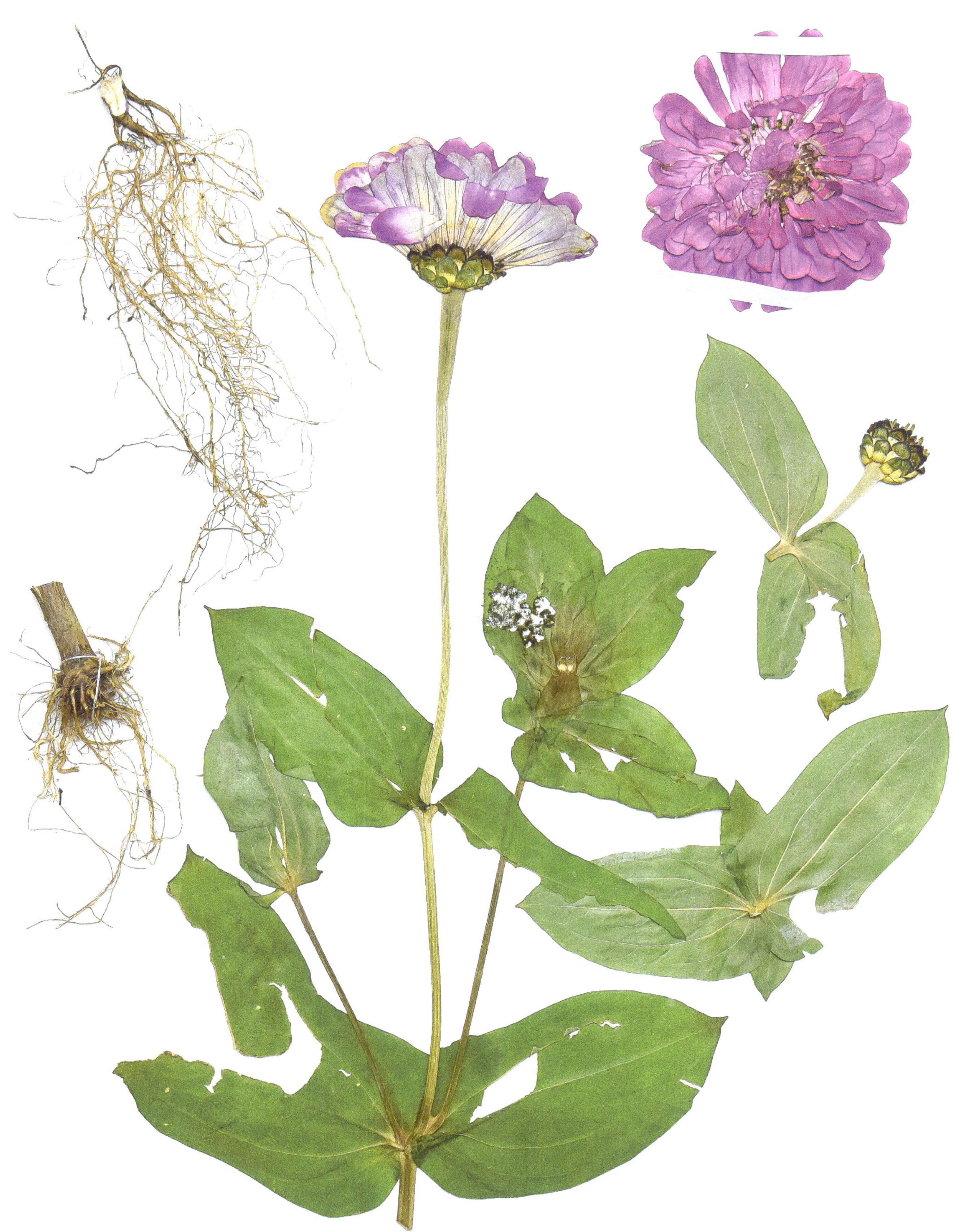

A Collection That is 100% Compostable

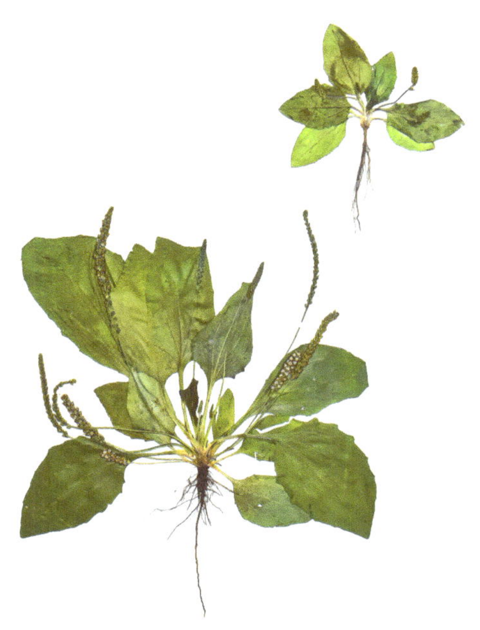

"One of the most tragic things I know about human nature is that all of us tend to put off living. We are all dreaming of some magical rose garden over the horizon instead of enjoying the roses that are blooming outside our windows today."

– Dale Carnegie

We know about the first herbarium (hortus siccus) only through references in books. It was started in the 16th century by Luca Ghini, professor of medicine and botany at the University of Pisa. Ghini is also credited with establishing Europe's first Botanical Garden.

Among the best-known plant collectors are Charles Darwin, Carl Linnaeus, and James Cook, but they likely had several assistants who remain uncredited for their work.

Often, information about the plants in a particular region comes from Indigenous cultures. Historically, Indigenous people were able to identify plants easily, which was crucial in determining which plants were edible and which were deadly. It is important to recognize the impact Indigenous people have had on the field of botany.

"When we know that we too are part of nature, we will take care of the earth"

- Heidi Hermary

The Essence of Organic Gardening

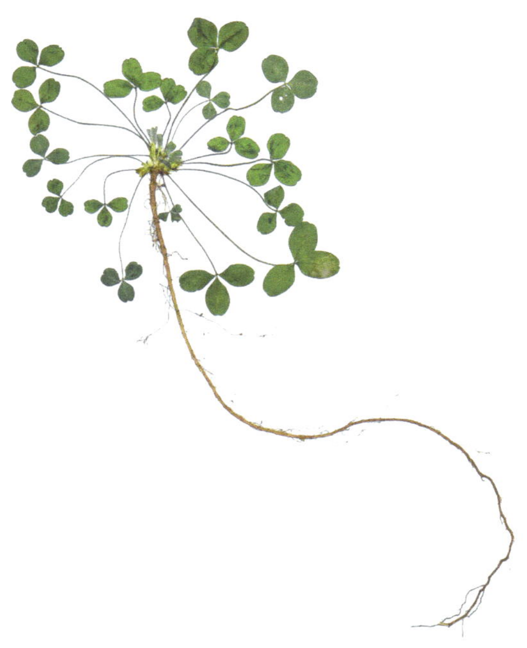

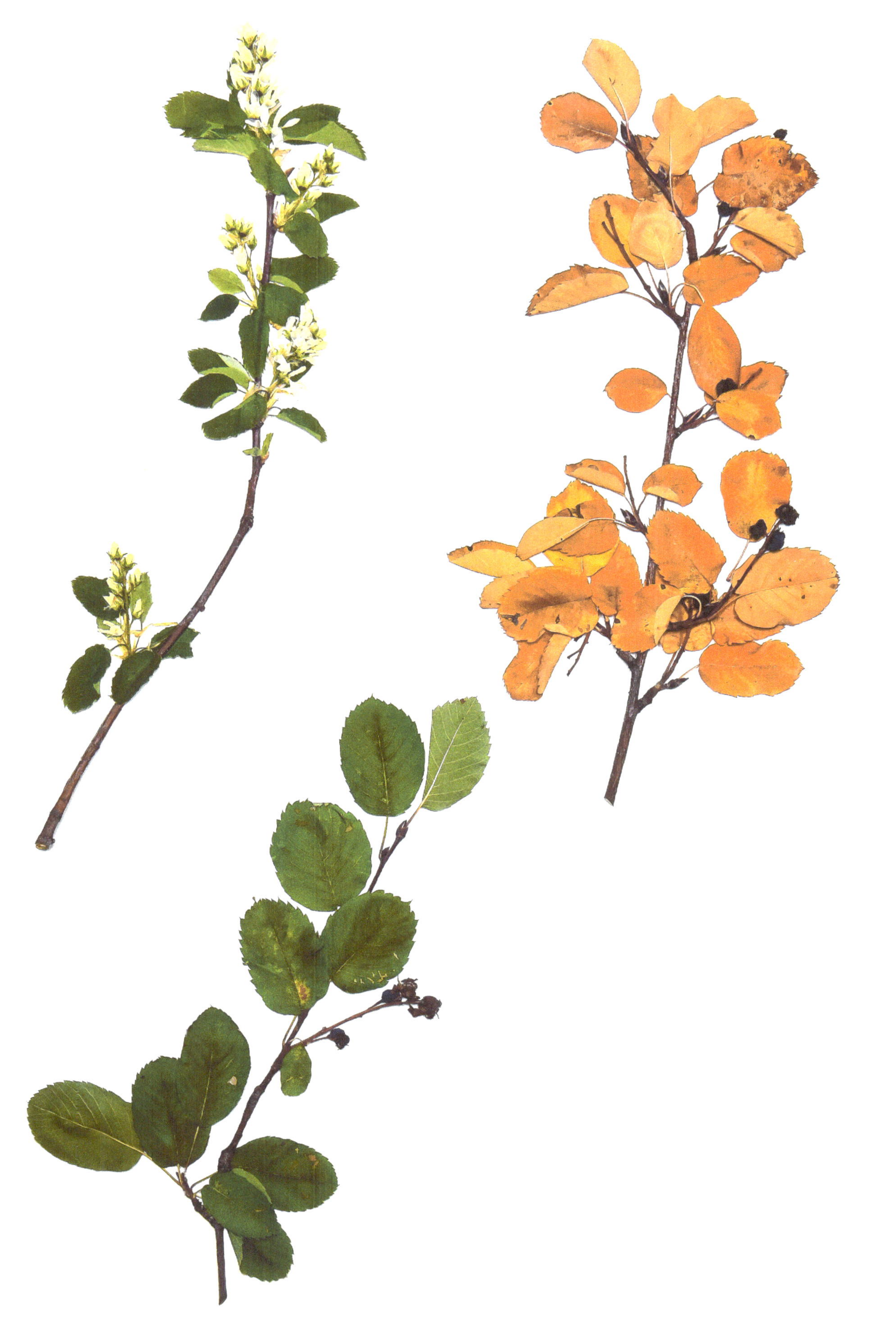

Help Nature Thrive

"To plant a garden is to believe in tomorrow."

– Audrey Hepburn

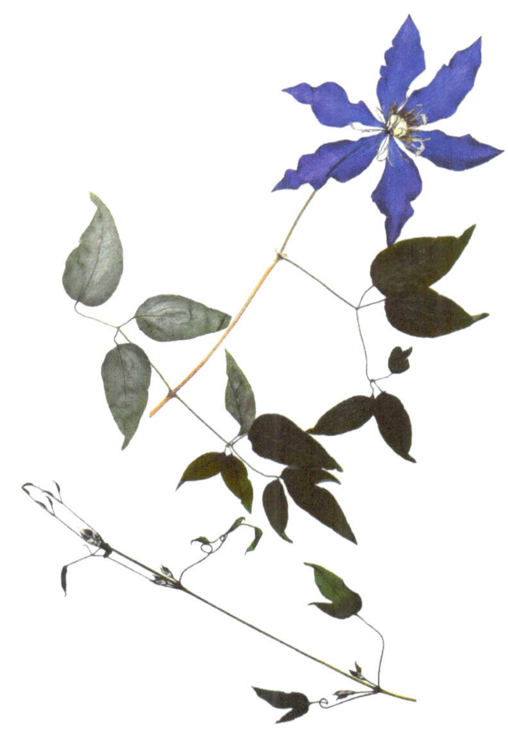

The Organic Master Gardener Program in Stony Plain has been hosted at the Multi-cultural Heritage Centre since 2007 and is Alberta's first and most extensive Organic Master Gardener Program. It is ideal for those who have a passion for gardening and want to expand their knowledge of botany, design, and soil sciences. It presents the big truths in plant health and earth care. In the program, students learn that the quality of their plants depends on the soil, and more importantly, the quality of their soil depends on their plants. Science has demonstrated that poor soil does not grow healthy plants and that many plant problems can be solved quite easily when we work with nature. The program's focus is on biology – growing soil, not plants, and using nature's own processes to control weeds, pests, and disease. Organic gardening embraces an ecological paradigm in all its practices.

Find Organic Master Gardener Program details at: www.multicentre.org/OMG

"Can you taste the difference between store-bought and home-grown? If that $12 salad has no flavour, then it's not food, it's just plants."
- Mark Stumpf-Allen

We can all be part of a just and healthy food system. It begins with a pack of seed and allowing nature to be your guide.

Bios

Mark Stumpf-Allen has been an instructor in the Organic Master Gardener Program since 2015 and assumed the role of Program Administrator in 2021. His family had a large urban vegetable garden in north-east Edmonton where he abandoned many rubber boots and socks that got stuck and lost in the heavy clay soil. After leaving home he began shopping for his vegetables rather than growing them and wondered why they just didn't taste as good. Upon moving into their home in the 90s, he and his husband Craig returned to home gardening, but discovered that getting a tasty crop from the depleted, chemically polluted urban soil was not as easy as it was from the old prairie soil of his youth.

His role as an educator began with his position managing a community garden, and then expanded when he worked for a decade as Edmonton's "Compost Doctor." As his knowledge of the soil sciences expanded, he turned his yard into a living laboratory, where he tests the latest hypotheses from leaders in regenerative agriculture to find out what works in our latitude and climate. One day, he hopes to know how to garden.

Alexis Marie Chute is a distinguished artist, photographer, filmmaker, art curator, and bestselling author. Her books include the fantasy trilogy *Above the Star, Below the Moon, Inside the Sun*, memoir *Expecting Sunshine: A Journey of Grief, Healing and Pregnancy After Loss*, and *Prairie Spirits: Ghost Stories & Hauntings at the Red Brick School and Oppertshauser House in Stony Plain, Alberta*. Her documentary films have screened around the world in countries such as Scotland, France, The Netherlands, and across the United States and Canada. She is the Art Curator at Wild Skies Art Gallery and the Multicultural Heritage Centre, and Founder-Curator of InFocus Photo Exhibit & Awards. Her artwork is represented by the Art Gallery of Alberta, Art Rental and Sales Program. **Contact Alexis Marie Chute: info@alexismariechute.com Find her online at www.AlexisMarieChute.com and on Instagram as @alexismariejoy**

Acknowledgements

The Heritage Agricultural Society appreciates the support of Devan Bailey, Shenae Borschneck, Amber Brennan, Janet Chalan, Georgina Coté, Alayna Dornbush, Kelly Dunn, Coleen Harman, Katie Ingram, Janice Sinclair, Jackie Skett, Tierra Stokes, Susan Walters, and Michelle White. Thank you for participating in the Organic Master Gardener program and for allowing us to photograph your herbariums for this book.

Many thanks to Mark Stumpf-Allen for the valuable perspectives shared in Eternal Summer. Mark, you were a wonderful collaborator and your energy and enthusiasm for this project—and all the work you do—was palpable and contagious.

Warm gratitude to Lorraine Taylor for her invaluable input, advice, and edits. Thank you, Lorraine, for the passionate work you do in horticulture.

Special thanks to the Donna Cherniawsky of the Royal Alberta Museum, Lauren MacLean with Government Records, Michael Dickie, and the George Pegg Botanic Garden Society for historic resources.

Thank you to the Multicultural Heritage Centre and the Government of Alberta for supporting this project. Thanks also to editor Jo Dawyd for your keen eye.

- Alexis Marie Chute, author, photographer, & publisher

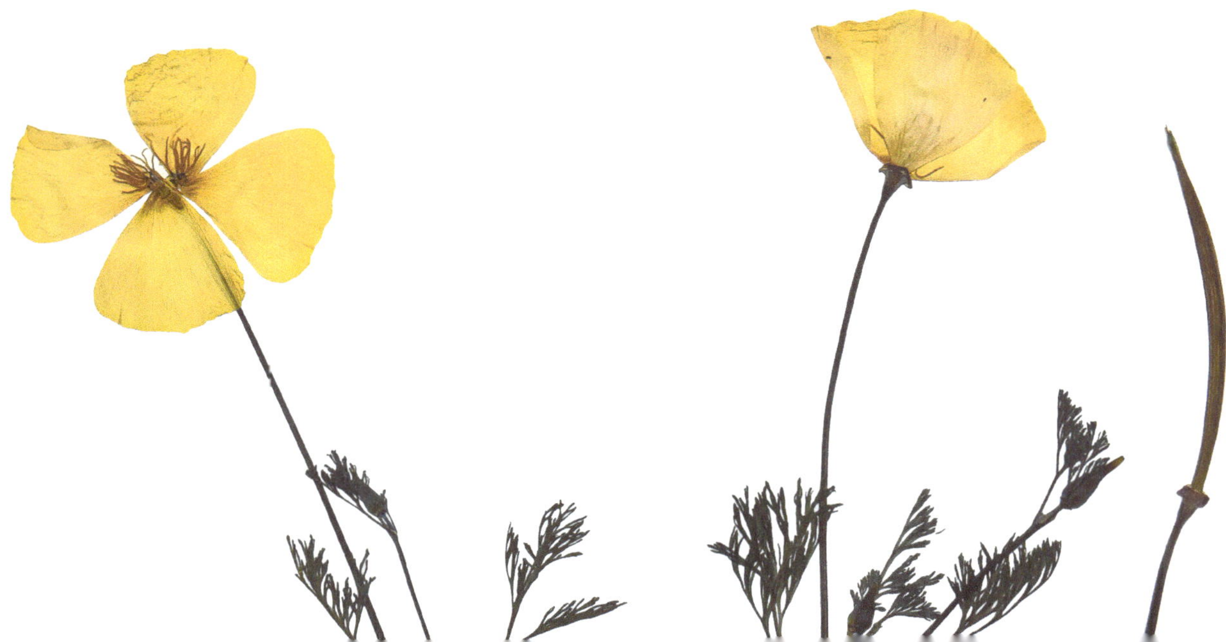

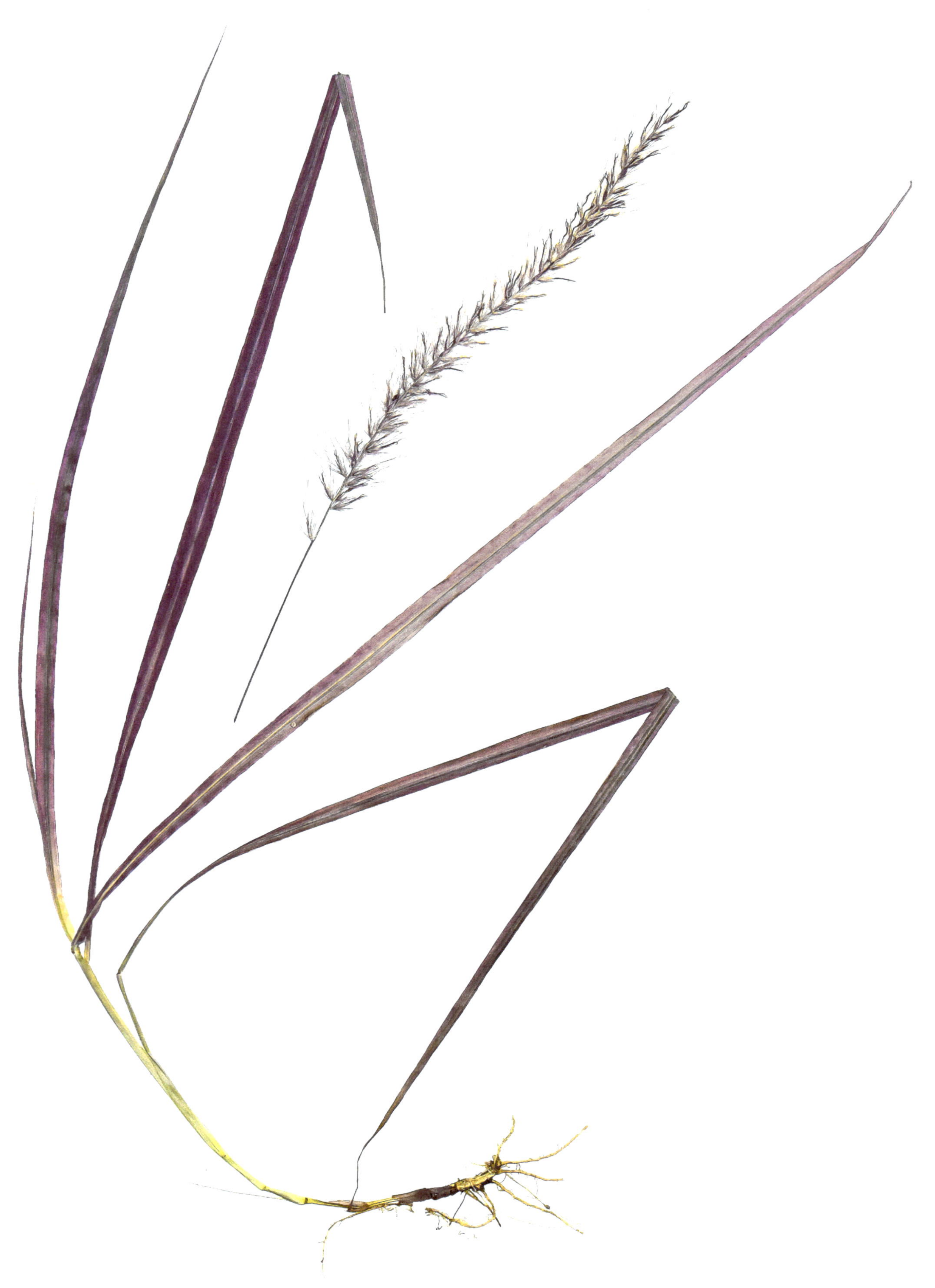

Herbariums in *Eternal Summer:*

Front Cover: Delphinium by G. Cote

Opening: False Sunflower (Heliopsis helianthoides) and Seaholly (Eryngium) from Karla
    Rippin's front yard

pg 3: Goutweed (Aegopodium podagraria 'Variegata') from Tierra Stokes' Stony Plain
    garden

pg 5: Grass (Poaceae) by Janet Chalán

pg 7: Lungwort (Pulmonaria soiccharata) by K. Rippin

pg 8: Rose from my Grandma's garden by Shenae Borschneck, showing harvesting by
    leafcutter bees

pg 9: Tickseed (Coreopsis verticillata) by K. Rippin

pg 10: White Clover (Trifolium repens), a cover crop from the MHC urban farm
    collected by Jackie Skett

pg 11: Anise Hyssop (Agastache foeniculum) collected in Parkland County by Katie
    Ingram

pg 12: Tansy (Tanacetum vulgare) by J. Chalán. The small envelope holds fragile plant
    parts and seeds.

pg 13: Sweet Pea (Lathyrus odoratus) by S. Borschneck

pg 14: Hosta by S. Borschneck whose collection reflects her relationship with her
    grandmother

pg 15: Dill (Anethum graveolens) collected by Georgina Coté

pg 17: Wooden plant press decorated with dried and pressed flowers

pg 19: Creeping Bellflower (Campanula rapunculoides) collected by Michelle White

pg 20: Lupin by S. Borschneck

pg 21: Wild or Prickly Rose (Rosa acicularis) collected in Westlock by Janice Sinclair

pg 22: Gayfeather (Liatris); collector unknown

pg 23: Artemisia by K. Ingram

pg 24: Purple Shamrock (Oxalis triangularis) a favourite houseplant of J. Skett

pg 25: Wild Buckwheat, (Polygonom convulvulus) that was growing amongst the juni-
pers in S. Walters' garden

pg 26: Jacob's Ladder (Polemonium caeruleum) by Alayna Dornbush

pg 27: Clematis 'Budapest' (Clematis integrifolia) that grows along the orchard fence in
    the Green and Gold Garden by J. Skett

pg 29: Lamb's Quarters (Chenopodium album) by M. White

pg 32: Common Groundsel (Senecio vulgaris) by T. Stokes

pg 39: Bleeding Heart (Lamprocapnos spectabilis) by J. Skett

pg 40: Rose blossoms from bud to bloom by G. Coté

pg 41: Comfrey (Symphytum officinale) by K. Ingram

Other Books by
Alexis Marie Chute

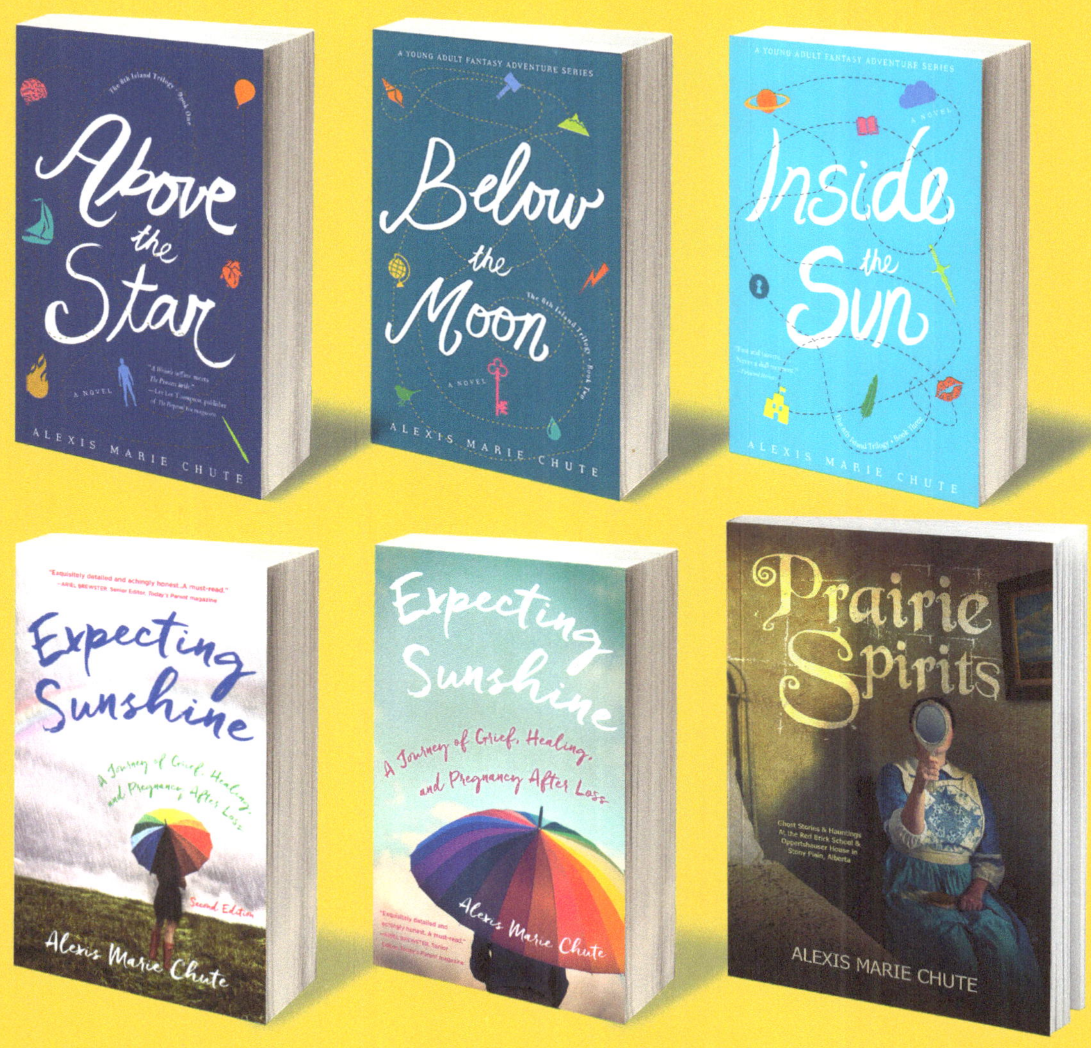

More information: www.AlexisMarieChute.com
& Wild Skies Press www.WildSkiesPress.com